When Our Blue Star Turned Gold

Terry A. Burgess

www.goldstarparent.com

Creative Team Publishing
Fort Worth, Texas

Disclaimers:
- Due diligence has been exercised to obtain written permission for use of references or quotes where required. Additional quotes or references may be subject to Fair Use Doctrine. Where additional references or quotes require source credit, upon written certification that such claim is accurate, credit for use will be noted on this website: www.goldstarparent.com
- The opinions and conclusions expressed are solely of the author and/or the individuals represented, and are limited to the facts, experiences, and circumstances involved. Certain names and related circumstances have been changed to protect confidentiality. All stories where names are mentioned are used with the permission of the parties involved. Any resemblance to past or current people, places, circumstances, or events is purely coincidental.

ISBN: 978-0-9979519-6-7

PUBLISHED BY CREATIVE TEAM PUBLISHING
www.CreativeTeamPublishing.com
Fort Worth, Texas
Printed in the United States of America

When Our Blue Star Turned Gold

Terry A. Burgess

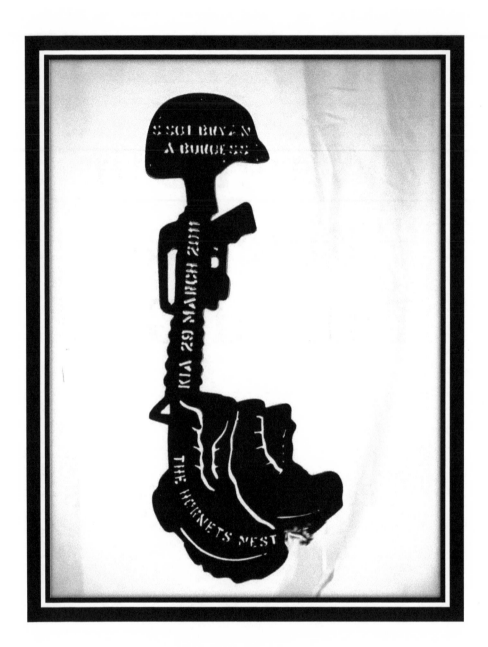

"Empty Boots"

~ Art creator wishes to remain anonymous

"On Behalf of a Grateful Nation..."

These are words no parent ever wants to hear. Becoming a Gold Star parent was never on our bucket list; yet, here we are, seven years later after being handed the flag that draped my son's casket.

We've been telling Bryan's story since that first horrible day, and though the heartbreak of Bryan's death has not lessened, the pain of sharing his story has changed from one of pure sorrow to one of honor and respect for his sacrifice. A parent who has lost a child will never "get over it." Grieving parents will move forward but never be able to "move on."

This book tells our ongoing journey of how we have dealt, and continue to deal with becoming grieving Gold Star parents, and keeping our sanity in a world that, for the most part, may not be entirely grateful for Bryan's sacrifice.

We have met some amazing, inspiring, and wonderful people on our journey, people we are proud to call patriots and friends. And while the statistics quoted say only one percent of the American population has ever served in the armed forces, we have discovered that this one percent produces a never-ending ripple effect. The United States Military has become our family; strangers have become friends.

Our hope is that this book will inform and educate those who are not Gold Stars while at the same time letting Gold Stars know it is okay to share their story and honor their sons and daughters who have given the ultimate sacrifice.

Though I use the term "Gold Star" throughout this book, I make no distinction between those killed in action, in training accidents, killed while on leave, suicides, or murders. I honor every son or daughter that has ever worn the "cloth of our nation."

Some grief counselors will tell you that "grief is linear with a light at the end of the tunnel." A grieving parent will tell you differently.

One of my favorite quotes is from Emily Dickinson's poem, *My Life Closed Twice Before Its Close*: "Parting is all we know of Heaven and all we need of Hell."

Children may have the opportunity to say goodbye to a dying parent, but when a parent is not given a chance to say goodbye to their child, they feel they have definitely been deprived of a crucial element of closure from death.

In our travels since that first flight to Dover AFB (Air Force Base) for Bryan's Dignified Transfer, our grief has taken many twists, turns, and different forms; from dreams to nightmares, from black-tie events in Dallas to mudding in Michigan, and from skydiving in Ohio to movie studios in Hollywood. And in every instance, we tell Bryan's story.

We would trade it all in the blink of an eye to have never had to experience any of it.

We are humbled and honored to share Bryan's story with you.

> We let Gold Stars know it is okay to share their story and honor their sons and daughters who have given the ultimate sacrifice.

Dedication

This book is dedicated to the parents who have lost a child who has served our country. We are members of a club no one wants to belong to.

We wear a pin that few Americans recognize. We carry a weight that is familiar to far too many Americans.

This book is for you and all who care about Gold Star Parents and Families, and who care deeply about sacrifice, honor, duty, and country.

And to our No Slack family, Bryan's brothers-in-arms and their families: you help us carry Bryan's name and his legacy forward every day, ensuring that he and all the fallen will never be forgotten. Mere words are not nearly sufficient enough to tell you how truly grateful we are and how much we love all of you.

Terry and Elisabeth Burgess
June, 2018

Acknowledgements

An immeasurable amount of love and gratitude goes to two very special women: my wife, Elisabeth, for her incredible support while we wrote this book, and to my son's wife and the mother of his children, Tiffany, who gave us strength of spirit and heart when ours was at its weakest.

Thank you, Glen Aubrey and the staff at Creative Team Publishing, for your enduring patience, support, and suggestions.

Thank you, Justin Aubrey, for designing the beautiful and striking cover.

Thanks to Randy Beck, www.mydomaintools.com for exceptional work on our website!

A very special "Thank you!" to everyone who has touched our lives since March 29, 2011. Our life is richer because of you.

Portrait

Staff Sergeant (SSG) Bryan A. Burgess

By Artist Phil Taylor

It still amazes me how Phil's portrait of Bryan can hold more depth of character than any photo of Bryan. I find myself just standing in front of the portrait, staring at Bryan's eyes. Would he be proud of everything we've done since his death? I will not know for sure until I see him again.

In 2014 we were introduced to The American Fallen Soldiers Project which was created by Phil and Lisa Taylor. Their organization provides original portraits of fallen soldiers to their families. Phil Taylor's portrait of Bryan hangs over our fireplace. The focal point of Phil's memorial portraits is the subject's eyes. The face and clothes are black, white, and gray. The American Flag in the background is red, white, and blue. The only other color in the portrait is in the eyes.

Bryan's portrait was presented to us at Christ Church on Altamesa Boulevard in Fort Worth, Texas on July 5, 2014. The presentations of the portraits are personalized for the families and become special events open to the public. As personal as our presentation was, we all received a surprising and amazing shock from one of the Honor Guard that stood on the stage by Bryan's portrait.

The Honor Guard leaned close to Beth and whispered to her that he was the one who had escorted Bryan home from Afghanistan on the Angel Flight to Dover. No one at the presentation knew that. He was so emotional about the presentation that he left the auditorium before I even had the chance to meet him and to thank him for bringing Bryan home. We have become good friends with the other Honor Guard that was there that day, John Alred, and have met him at several other events.

The presentation was filmed and became part of Phil Taylor's special series *Brush of Honor* on INSP TV. Viewers can watch Bryan's episode on YouTube at *Brush of Honor – Bryan Burgess* and also on INSP.com/Bryan.

~ Use of the original portrait of Staff Sgt. Bryan Burgess
is granted by Phil Taylor, Artist
Founder The American Fallen Soldiers Project
Painting Copyright © 2014. All Rights Reserved.
The American Fallen Soldiers Project
https://americanfallensoldiers.com

Endorsements on behalf of
When Our Blue Star Turned Gold

*****
~ David Salzberg, Jr. and Christian Tureaud
Executive Producers and Directors of *The Hornet's Nest*

"We met Terry and Beth Burgess not long after their beloved son, Army Staff Sergeant Bryan Burgess, was killed in action while serving with the 101st Airborne in Afghanistan during 2011. The families who lose a loved one in combat all handle this devastating news differently. Terry and Beth used the love and loss of Bryan to help others through truly selfless acts.

"The tireless effort that Terry and Elisabeth Burgess put toward helping families in the Gold Star community is second to none and a big part of the inspiration for us to continue making the *Heroes of Valor* film collection. The Burgess family shows us how to do something amazing and positive from a very tough situation. We love them and they are real heroes just like Bryan."

*****

~ Joy Stevens, Major General,
Texas National Guard, Retired
Founder of the Texas War Memorial
~ Colonel (Ret.) James M. Stryker
Chairman, Texas War Memorial
http://texaswarmemorial.com/

"As Americans we do not really understand the sacrifices made by our military families. The service member and their entire family serve. Although their family is not in the combat zone, their heart and soul are there with their service member until their service member returns. The sacrifice of parents of fallen service members is the most overlooked burden that they carry for the rest of their lives. A spouse may have the difficult and sad opportunity to secure a new spouse but a parent cannot replace a lost child who they brought into the world, nurtured, and raised. Those special dreams a parent shares of that child's future, are lost forever.

"Terry and Beth Burgess have done it with class. They have worked diligently with the Texas War Memorial to place a monument on the Texas Capital Grounds to honor all service members and their families that have served since 9/11. Their dedication to help and serve the other families reflects their character and that of all military families. They are imbued with a strong desire to serve our nation. Thank you to all service members and their families."

*****

~ Casey D. McEuin, President and Executive Director
Project RELO
www.projectrelo.org

"The Burgesses have experienced loss that no parent should ever have to suffer. They have endured with a level of grace and altruism that is commendable. Through shared experience, what they have done to honor the legacy of their fallen warrior is nothing short of amazing.

"This book allows the reader to learn the deep understanding of what a Blue Star Family prays will never happen, and how a Gold Star Family copes with the realization of their loss."

*****

~ Karl Monger, Executive Director
GallantFew, Inc.
www.gallantfew.org

"Beth and Terry Burgess are Gold Star parents. In elementary school a Gold Star is the highest achievement. In this sense, however, it is the most awful distinction a person can receive, for it means they have lost a son or daughter in service to our nation, paying the price for our freedom with their very life. I can imagine nothing worse to happen than the death of a loved one, and a Gold Star family member should be among the highest honored and well cared for in our society. Sadly, this is not the case. Most Americans have no idea, and that means resources are few and far between.

"For Terry, the pain nearly caused him to end his own life. Fortunately, Beth and Terry found purpose in sacrifice and set out to provide a safe, healing space for other Gold Star family members. *When Our Blue Star Turned Gold* honors their son and tells their story from devastating loss to providing hope and healing."

A veteran reading this may experience the re-opening of wounds suppressed. If that has happened to you, don't internalize and keep that to yourself. Connect with a veteran network such as GallantFew. GallantFew has support resources to help with emotional and physical pain that don't involve drugging you or making you talk through your experiences. The greatest threat to your future is isolation. Join the community. Contact GallantFew. www.gallantfew.org.

Order **Common Sense Transition** by Karl Monger at:

https://gallantfew.org/store/common-sense-transition/

~ Terry Burgess and Karl Monger

*****

~ Tempa Sherrill M.S., LPC
Chief Clinical Officer, 22KILL
www.22KILL.com

"In 2016 I went to a screening of *The Hornet's Nest*. Afterwards, I had the privilege of hearing the most heartfelt words of love and devotion coming from the parents of one of the fallen soldiers in the documentary.

"As tears streamed down my face, I instantly knew that our souls were meant to connect. Terry and Beth Burgess have been an inspiration to me personally and to many others. Their unwavering passion for honoring their son, Bryan, and his teammates, serves as motivation to keep going.

"Their story is a model to others that healing is possible if you are willing to put one foot in front of the other. I am honored to march beside them in the veteran community in serving those families who too often feel left behind.

"*When Our Blue Star Turned Gold* is a message of sacrifice, pain, and resilience that all Americans need to hear to truly understand that freedom isn't free."

*****

Introduction

This book is seven years in the making. I've had to rely on my faulty memory and some social media posts to get the events in the right order, and I apologize if I have mixed up any days and/or people who attended a particular function.

As you read through the book, you will notice that some events will lead back to a previous event or jump forward to another 'future memory.' This is what it's like to have 'grief brain.' Thoughts are fragmented and the past looks like a fractal pattern which resulted from having my life—past, present, and future—shattered in an instant.

Beth recalls a dinner a group of us attended at Texas Road House on our second night in Dover. She remembers who was there and even a conversation the group had with the waitperson.

I have absolutely no recollection at all of that dinner.

I used to keep a daily journal. The day Bryan was killed I stopped taking notes of my day-to-day life. Putting that event and the following days into words meant that Bryan's death was real. Putting it all on paper made it permanent.

Even when the U.S. Army mailed us the official report of the battle that claimed Bryan's life, I did not open the envelope. I literally threw the package into the trunk that now contained Bryan's life. I stood over the trunk, looking at the *things* that represented my son's service to our country.

One recurring thought ran through my mind: *how can I live up to my son's sacrifice?*

This book, this story, in ink and on paper, tells how we as a Gold Star family did just that. Now, at the end of each day, I ask myself one question: *Would Bryan be proud of what I did today?*

I still have not read the official Army report about the day Bryan was killed. I've talked to enough of the men who were right there with him that I know exactly what happened and why. And I know I can never change it.

What I have been able to change is the way I have handled the worst day of my life. That day was not just twenty-four hours; it consumes every waking moment and it is sometimes a haunting dream.

> What I have been able to change is the way I have
> handled the worst day of my life.

Dark thoughts invade whenever friends and family fail to understand the impact losing my son has had on my life. Reliving that day, and the following days, weeks, months, and years, and putting them into words, have been extremely difficult and at times overwhelmingly emotional.

As conflicting as it sounds, meeting other Gold Star parents and listening to their heartbreaking and sometimes overwhelmingly tragic stories lets us know that we are not alone in our never-ending journey of grief.

Even though our story begins in 2011 and is now a few years old, the issue of dealing with the deaths of our sons and daughters will remain contemporary as long as there are wars.

My son knew exactly why he was volunteering to go to war. To this day I wonder how well young people understand the true cost of war and if there are some that feel the tug of patriotism in their heart and soul like Bryan did.

Foreword by US Army SFC Michael Schlitz, Retired

~ The Author with Michael Schlitz at Sky Ball XIII,
Dallas, Texas, October 24, 2015

I first met the Burgess family back in 2014 while on a business trip to Los Angeles. I had been invited to attend a private screening of the documentary *The Hornet's Nest*. I had heard the documentary was coming out soon and that it was based on a unit in the 101st Airborne Division during their deployment to Afghanistan. What I got that night was more than I ever expected.

I watched *The Hornet's Nest* with a room full of Veterans, Veteran supporters, film crew, and, of course, some of the Gold Star Families. I can remember being introduced to Terry Burgess after the screening and immediately made the connection that he was the Gold Star Father of Army SSG Bryan Burgess. He was warm, inviting, and spoke freely about his experiences, losing his son. I was drastically injured in Iraq in 2007 and having over 90 surgeries, I stood there in awe of Terry's strength.

Over the last several years I have had the good fortune to run into both Terry and his beautiful wife, Gold Star Mother Elisabeth, many times. Usually at a Veteran based event that we're both supporting, each time taking a moment to speak with them about their journey, their strength, and their commitment. I think it's obvious where their passion to giving back to the Veteran Community comes from, but to listen to their story is remarkable.

Both Terry and Elisabeth remain as an inspiration to me for their passionate, loving, and gracious hearts and for having the dedication and courage to tell their story, carry on Bryan's legacy, and support the Veteran and Gold Star communities. I know the emails, phone calls, and friendship will carry on for years to come.

Thank you, Terry and Elisabeth. I hope this book will help preserve Bryan's legacy and bring inspiration to people around the world. I am forever changed because of you.

Foreword by
Master Sergeant Blair Anderson, Retired

"Bryan's Gift"

Introduction by the Author: "Blair Anderson met Bryan on a mountaintop right before Operation Strong Eagle III.

"Blair said he and Bryan talked for less than fifteen minutes. Seven years later, Blair recalls that conversation vividly. He told me he thinks of the conversation as 'Bryan's Gift.'"

*****

It was a busy morning, that mid-March day back in 2011.

Task Force No Slack, the 101st Airborne Regiment's battalion then stationed in Kunar Province, Afghanistan, was preparing for a convoy support action called an overwatch mission. This one was called "Bastogne Overwatch XV," or "BOW Fifteen." My impression of it was that it was reminiscent of scenes out of the movie *The Road Warrior*. The overwatch missions were our way of prepositioning troops along a route where a convoy would later pass, creating as safe a corridor as we could for other trucks, including civilian vehicles, to deliver their much-needed supplies to some of the most austere forward installations found in the U.S. military.

But in order to establish that protection, we ourselves had to first secure them. And this was along a notorious route in Kunar Province called Main Supply Route CALIFORNIA.

We first flew up in UH-60 Blackhawk helicopters from Forward Operating Base (FOB) Joyce to Combat Outpost Monti, where we would embed ourselves with the platoons already there before going "outside the wire" and into Taliban-held land. As it was my first combat mission, I had no idea what to expect. I was a 39-year-old Air Force Technical Sergeant, an E-6, and despite my prior Army service I had no combat experience whatsoever; most of my work had been done from the comfort of a desk inside a large base or facility.

Upon arrival at Monti, 101st Airborne Soldiers directed us to the Tactical Operations Center, where we were told to await further instruction. This gave us approximately 30 minutes to reflect on what was about to happen.

It was time I didn't want.

I now had time to think about all the things that could happen, and I had learned to be apprehensive of the unknown. Waiting, therefore, could sometimes be a Soldier's mind's worst enemy. At least it certainly was to this old Soldier-Airman.

My team leader and I conducted one last pre-mission check, and suddenly I found myself without anything else to do. I stood there looking around as all the other Soldiers gathered themselves in the hallway, plunking down rucksacks and weapons and finding a place to sit. As far as I knew, I was the only Airman there, even though I found out later there were a couple others, known as Joint Terminal Air Controllers — JTACs.

One 101st Soldier came through and placed his gear against the other wall from me, but instead of sitting like the others he stood and looked around. I saw that he was also an E-6, an Army Staff Sergeant, and I felt a little relieved that we were the same rank. I cracked a joke, something innocuous, and he turned and laughed a little before adding his own little joke.

Normally, we Airmen wouldn't make small-talk with the Army Soldiers present; many of them were either silent professionals or chatty buddies, each emblazoned with various patches: the 'Screaming Eagle' of the 101st along with 'Airborne,' 'Ranger,' or 'Scout,' or something equally vaunted. But something about this Staff Sergeant standing across from me put me at ease.

I'm not sure if he noticed my nerves about the upcoming mission, but we started talking and he told me what to expect. He was easy to get along with, subdued, humble, and professional, and I reminded myself that I should start remembering names. I looked at his name tab and saw the name: BURGESS. "Burgess Meredith," I thought, from the *Rocky* movies. I wouldn't forget him.

About fifteen minutes later, somebody came through and barked an order to move out to the motor pool to board our vehicles. Staff Sergeant Burgess and I went off in our own directions.

I had no idea those fifteen minutes would change my life, or that it was the beginning of a much bigger gift. What began as a simple consolation of a jittery Soldier-Airman would branch out down the road.

Although the overwatch mission produced casualties, no one died and the 101st got even closer to going home.

Two weeks later, though, and roughly two weeks before he was slated to go home, Staff Sergeant Bryan Burgess was gone. He and five other Soldiers lost their lives during an operation called Strong Eagle III with a further seven or so wounded and about two dozen others suffering from rough terrain and cold weather-related injuries.

Even though I didn't directly participate on that mission, I helped monitor the radios in the Operations Center on FOB Joyce and could hear what was going on all during that first few days. It was grim, and the commotion was incredible.

By the end of the operation, which lasted nine days versus the three days planned, over 120 Taliban were confirmed killed and a further 68 taken into custody.

But something changed. Our FOB Joyce, was safe, quiet. Whereas before I had counted eight attacks over my first fourteen days on the FOB, no attacks occurred for several weeks. FOB Joyce, I found, would not be attacked by the Taliban until after the last 101st Soldier went home. Bryan and his fellow Soldiers had left us something precious: immediate safety to those of us staying behind.

Kunar Province eventually returned to its dangerous state over time but some six months later, my buddy and I finally started on our way home. We had made it out alive, and the journey home grew more exciting the closer we got. The day we could only dream of — once a pipe dream during fitful, sleepless nights of worrying whether we'd ever make it out alive — was now within reach and growing closer. We went through Bagram. Kyrgyzstan. Turkey. Germany. And then — finally — the United States.

The fanfare around us moved us when we got back: a long line of people greeted us at Baltimore-Washington International Airport, giving us gifts and well-wishes; people thanked us; they insisted on buying our lunches or coffees in the terminals; the stateside civilian airlines gave us the chance to get off first; and my family and chain-of-command all greeted us at the airport at Denver.

It was one of the best days of my life.

Yet, although it was an amazing welcome home after such a hard deployment, the trumpets soon faded while the memories of combat, attacks on the FOB, and friends lost remained. People busied themselves with everyday life and I went back to work. I went on to a new desk position, tested for my next rank, and prepared to go to Noncommissioned Officer Academy, all within weeks and months of coming home. It was almost as if the deployment didn't matter. And because I was an Individual Augmentee during my deployment, I had very few, if any, people around me who could relate.

The silence, at times, was deafening. I even tried to tell my wife about what it was like, but she and others close to me opted to not hear about something so dangerous or dark. I was told at certain points to perhaps seek counseling, but to me I didn't like the thought of talking to other strangers who didn't know me or what I'd been through. And I still had to be a dad, a husband, and now Master Sergeant Anderson through it all.

Against my own yearnings, I slowly retreated into a shell and started suppressing my memories. I did my best to focus my energies in a positive way and I spent as much time as I could with my family. My son was born almost a year later and I did my best to be a good father. I clung to them and shunned spending my time with anybody else because I felt I had missed so much time with them and was so close — on more occasions than I'd cared to count — to not seeing them again.

The immediate things that I worried about — protecting life and limb — were no longer needed. Now, "important" things were not answering emails in a timely fashion, or taking training or responding to Air Force "taskers" before their due dates, or properly filling out performance reports to somebody else's exacting standard. My frustration grew. Those around me noticed I was a little more aggressive, even more sensitive, after coming home, and I knew that I needed to staunch whatever it was inside me. Over time and with some effort I began to fall back in line with civilization.

Still, I felt … different.

Then, one night in the spring of 2014, nearly three years after my deployment, I asked my wife to see the movie, *Lone Survivor*. Although it was mainly a loose account of something that had happened in Afghanistan, I thought it was a way of showing her—through somebody else's, even Hollywood's, eyes—what it was like to be there. We saw it, she expressed shock, but we didn't talk about it much.

To me, though, the movie brought back all sorts of memories and I started reminiscing. Late that night, I started searching on the Internet for ABC News reporter Mike Boettcher's stories from Kunar Province during my time out there, especially regarding Operation Strong Eagle III, because the mountaintop that had been mentioned in the movie was somewhere in the province. I wanted to know how close I got to that location, if I did at all, and a quick search on Google Earth found Showkay Gar—exactly seven miles from where I had been on one mission. And it was in the background of a picture I had taken once, from far up a hillside along the Pech River.

I was stunned.

I dug even further.

In my searches, though, I started finding links and references to a movie called *The Hornet's Nest*, a full-feature documentary about the Marines and the Army's 101st Airborne in Afghanistan that was due for release later that year. I clicked on one of them and was shocked to see the very memorial I attended with my buddies on FOB Joyce, honoring the six soldiers who perished on Strong Eagle III in an early movie trailer. My initial assumption was that the story of the 101st and Strong Eagle III would be lost to the ages, and it fed my hunger to find out more.

I reached out to the movie's Web page, and there I found Terry Burgess — Bryan's father.

Excited but apprehensive, I had to say something about those fifteen minutes I spent with Bryan. I was worried, because I wasn't in the "band of brothers" that he and his fellow soldiers were in together; I just wasn't one of them. They'd suffered through long deployments to some of the worst places in Iraq and Afghanistan together. They took care of each other, knew each other, knew each other's families, and shared a bond I could only dream of. I was a nobody, coming out of nowhere, and with very little to say other than "I was there" and "I met your son once."

Then something wonderful happened. Terry reached back to me. He heard me. He understood. And then he introduced me to his wife, Elisabeth, and Bryan's mother, Linda. We became fast friends, and my family met Terry and Elisabeth over dinner while we moved on a Permanent Change of Station from Denver to San Antonio later that summer.

That was in 2014, and my relationship to Bryan's family grew stronger. We shared stories. We talked by phone. We kept in touch through social media. Terry and Elisabeth came down to attend my retirement ceremony from the Air Force in San Antonio in June of 2018, and ended up staying longer than anticipated because of how well everybody got along. It was a weekend I will forever cherish.

For me, it was cathartic.

At my ceremony, I had asked Terry to deliver a few words to the audience about his son's life because I didn't want the event to just be about my retirement; I wanted it to be about all the wonderful people I'd met during my career, and to honor all those who had made the ultimate sacrifice during my time in service. From my first joining the Army in late 1990 to my eventual retirement from the Air Force in 2018, some 8,000-plus lives were lost during that time span over three wars and numerous operations, and Bryan—Staff Sergeant Burgess—was but one of them. Yet, to me, his existence, his calm demeanor, his professionalism, and his love of country and family changed my life. I wanted them to hear his story.

Now, several more officers, enlisted members, and civilians will honor and remember him, and they will pay tribute to the Gold Star Family who raised him to be the great American he turned out to be.

As for me, it finally allowed me the chance to talk about what I'd been through with people who understood, whereas before I felt I had no one.

That weekend Bryan's gift—like a tree offering comforting shade and protection—had branched. Many others have been touched and brought together. Families were joined in love, fun, and understanding. And my mind has finally found time to rest.

All because of a Brother in Arms I had barely met.

Table of Contents

Table of Contents

Table of Contents

*****

*****

~ Staff Sergeant (SSG) Bryan A. Burgess
Afghanistan, November, 2010
Photograph by Sergeant Nate Allen

Chapter 1
The Dream that Started It All

Operation Strong Eagle III into Kunar Province, Afghanistan was Bryan's third deployment. While he was deployed into Afghanistan, I had a dream about him. In the dream, Bryan and I are walking side by side on a rocky, dusty, dirt road.

Bryan was dressed in full combat uniform and he was talking to me, but I couldn't hear what he was saying to me. He had no voice.

He smiled at me, took me by the elbow and guided me around a corner into an outdoor movie theater. We took our seats and there on the movie screen appeared Bryan in his Army Combat Uniform.

The camera pulled back and I could see he was standing beside a glass coffin. He stepped into the coffin, laid down, and as soon as his helmet touched the white satin pillow he turned into my little boy Bryan. Little boy Bryan sat up, stepped out of the coffin, and became Bryan the soldier again. Bryan gave me a sharp salute, that crooked half-smile I was so familiar with, and then the screen went blindingly white. I turned to look at Bryan in the seat beside me, but he was gone.

It was at that point that I woke up to the phone ringing. It was my daughter-in-law, Tiffany, telling me that Bryan had been killed in action in Afghanistan early that morning.

It was 7:00 am on March 29, 2011, and our entire world had just been shattered.

I remember telling Tiffany, "I just saw him. I just dreamed about him. I just saw him." Through her sobbing gasps for air, Tiffany told us an Army colonel and chaplain were at her house right then, and that we could expect a similar visit at any time that morning. If there had been any possible way to physically reach through the phone line to embrace Tiffany in a hug, I would have done it right then.

Tiffany told us later that when she received her notification, Makya, her daughter, ran into the front room to see why her mother had screamed. Tiffany does not remember screaming.

After Tiffany hung up, Beth called her sister, Fran, and Beth I walked down to her sister's house. Fran lived only three houses down from us, and she was already bawling when she opened the door. I think Beth and I spent an hour or so there while they called family members. I was already in the daze that would consume me for the next several weeks.

For some reason, while Beth and Fran were calling our families, I left Fran's house and walked back home. I arrived at the same time as U.S. Army Lieutenant Colonel Eberhart, and Reverend Mark Moore from the Grace Lutheran Church just down the street, arrived at our house. I invited them in, offered them something to drink, doing anything to delay the inevitable. LTC Eberhart looked me in the eyes, and said, "The United States Army regrets to inform you..."

I thought I was ready to hear that.

I immediately started weeping. Not just crying, but full-on weeping. I had cried at the deaths of grandparents, aunts, uncles, even pets. But I had never, ever wept like this. Rev. Moore held me in a comforting hug as the lieutenant colonel finished his speech. I don't even remember what else the lieutenant colonel, or the chaplain, said to me.

It was maybe an hour or so later that Beth returned home. She told me family was on the way. The phone rang, startling both of us. Neither of us really wanted to ever again touch that wretched device. Beth answered and told me it was Sergeant First Class (SFC) Newton Rose from Fort Hood who had been assigned to us as our Casualty Assistance Officer (C.A.O.). I talked to him briefly, and he told me he would be at our house later that day.

In the meantime, family members began to arrive at our home.

Our house is not small, but we don't have a large one, either. Family soon filled our home with soft chatter, tearful hugs, and from somewhere, the aroma of pizza. Beth's cousin, Dan, had bought pizza for everyone. I remember seeing Beth's sisters, her nieces and nephews, cousins, my younger brother, Lynn, and his wife, Ranae, milling around the house, talking softly to each other but no one speaking directly to me. Dan offered me a piece of pizza, but there was no way on earth I could chew and swallow anything. I took Dan aside and told him about my dream of Bryan that morning, asking him what he thought it might mean. He hugged me tightly and said, "In time, you will know."

Several months passed before I did know.

Our CAO arrived that afternoon. Our phone rang and it was SFC Rose asking if we were the house with the huge rosemary bush out front. We were. I met him at the door, invited him into our home, and looked into the eyes of a man that almost immediately became family. A computer could not have matched us with a more perfect CAO. SFC Rose was also a chef, and he admired our rosemary bush for its culinary value. We admired SFC Rose for his personal value to us. He volunteered to be a CAO knowing that he would be facing us on the worst day of our entire lives, and he did so with exacting dignity, grace, and honor, not only to us, but to Bryan.

After some minor introductory talk, he told us exactly what to expect over the next few days and weeks. To say that he took us by the hand would be an understatement. He told us that the first thing to expect was a flight to Dover AFB (Air Force Base) for Bryan's Dignified Transfer. After he explained it to us, I translated it as *my boy is coming home for the last time.*

From the Talking Proud website:

> "A dignified transfer is the process by which, upon the return from the theater of operations to the United States, the remains of Fallen military members are transferred from the aircraft to a waiting vehicle and then to the port mortuary. The dignified transfer is not a ceremony; rather, it is a solemn movement of the transfer case by a carry team of military personnel from the Fallen member's respective service. A dignified transfer is conducted for every U.S. military member who dies in the theater of operation while in the service of their country. A senior ranking officer of the Fallen

member's service presides over each dignified transfer.

"The sequence of the dignified transfer starts with the Fallen being returned to Dover by the most expedient means possible, which may mean a direct flight from theater, or a flight to Ramstein Air Base, Germany, and then to Dover. It is the Department of Defense's policy, and AFMAO's mission, to return America's Fallen to their loved ones as quickly as possible. Once the aircraft lands at Dover, service-specific carry teams remove the transfer cases individually from the aircraft and move them to a waiting mortuary transport vehicle. Once all of the transfer cases have been taken to the transport vehicles, they are then taken to the port mortuary."

~ http://www.talkingproud.us/Military/Dignified
Transfer/DignifiedTransfer/MortuaryAffairs.html

I asked Sgt. Rose if there were others killed in the battle that claimed Bryan. He told us the mission was ongoing and that he did not have any information at that time that he could disclose to us. We didn't press him any further.

Sgt. Rose was staying at a nearby hotel, and he told us to be packed and ready to fly to Dover as soon as possible. We packed but I don't remember what, and sure enough Sgt.

Rose called and said the flight was to leave the next afternoon.

On the flight to Dover, I was in the window seat, Beth was in the middle, and a businessman sat in the aisle seat. The usual in-flight conversation began between Beth and the businessman about where we were headed and why. Beth told him exactly where and why. The businessman just did not know how to reply to Beth. With tears in his eyes he offered to buy us something to eat and drink, and we graciously accepted some Pringles and sodas even though we didn't feel like eating. Beth says that this was our first encounter and experience as Gold Star parents. It was a shocking realization for all of us about how different a path our life was now taking.

We learned very quickly that the term "sad-bombed" used by military survivors is very apropos. We never do it intentionally, but over the last few years we've learned not to shy away from telling Bryan's story to someone because the story itself is a valuable teaching tool when it comes to the general population.

We arrived in Dover to a rainy, cold night. We had not packed warm clothes or an umbrella, but when the van we were in pulled up to the Fisher House where we were staying on base, a half dozen people with umbrellas met us at the driveway and escorted us inside.

Fisher House for the Fallen is one of those organizations that I hope no one ever, ever needs. It is a mansion on base at Dover AFB that literally caters to families of fallen soldiers. The house is as comfortable and comforting as it is beautiful. Completely operated by volunteers, it became "home" for us for the next two days.

Fisher House is where I met Frank Adamski for the first time. His son, SSG Frank Adamski, III was killed in the same battle as Bryan. We learned there were four more families on the way to Dover.

We were all exhausted, but terribly restless, of course. Tiffany and her CAO arrived and she told me that she had some details she needed to discuss with Bryan's family, but that she needed lots of caffeine before tackling that chore. Her CAO, Sgt. Steed, volunteered to drive us off base to a Starbucks. We piled back into the van and drove into downtown Dover to a Kroger grocery store that had a Starbucks. Sgt. Steed parked at one entrance and as we entered the store we could see the Starbucks clear at the other end. Sgt. Steed is a good-sized soldier and he led us like a platoon down to the Starbucks, clearing customers in front of us like the Red Sea.

I got my cup of coffee and walked over to Sgt. Steed who was now sitting on a bench, his cover in his hands and his head bowed. I honestly thought he was praying. He looked up as I approached and I offered to get him something to drink. He declined, saying that he appreciated my offer but that he was only there for us, for Bryan's family.

It was to be a very long night.

Most nights as I lay in bed my brain wants to replay my entire life. That night, I let it run.

*****

A year after 9/11 Bryan came to us and told us, "I'm going to fight back."

He wasn't asking our permission, he was telling us. The fact was that he had already enlisted with the U.S. Army to become an infantryman. Beth and I had watched 9/11 unfold on the T.V. as had most of America. We had co-workers in Garden City New York that could see the smoke pouring from the Twin Towers downtown.

There was no doubt that Bryan would go to war. He was determined to fight the enemy that had killed American citizens on American soil.

We gave him a tearful blessing.

Bryan was in boot camp at Fort Benning, Georgia. He made a connection almost immediately; his drill sergeant was from Spring, Texas, not too far north of Cleburne where Bryan had been born and raised.

Bryan's letters home told us that he was going to be okay. He was making extra cash by polishing the other cadet's shoes to a perfect shine.

Bryan had been a pitcher for the Cleburne Little League so when it came to time to learn how to lob a grenade, he had no problem hitting the target each time. He earned his grenade badge in record time.

The day came for the cadet's introduction to CS-Gas, a nasty, debilitating gas that will wrack your lungs, burn your eyes, and practically destroy your nasal passages. Bryan had a severe sinus infection that day. He told us later that the CS-Gas had completely cleared his sinuses and he felt so much better after being in the gas chamber. I told him I didn't think that was how the exercise was supposed to go.

Bryan excelled at most everything the Army trained him for, except putting up with his glasses. His vision was poor enough that he had to have corrective lenses. The Army didn't allow him to wear contacts so they provided him with Army-issue glasses. They were these huge, square-framed, black rimmed, goggle-like monsters that he was forced to wear. The first thing he asked me after his graduation at boot camp was to go get some new glasses. We all took off for the local mall and found a one-hour vision center that soon had Bryan back in some very stylish frames. He told us his face felt ten pounds lighter!

I feel bad about it now, but for Bryan's Welcome Home from boot camp, I had purchased these gag glasses that looked like the ones he had to wear, along with a bunch of toy Army helmets for everyone to wear. Bryan was gracious enough to laugh when he saw all of us wearing the glasses and helmets, but I wonder if he thought I was just making fun of him.

We attended his graduation from Boot Camp and I remember searching the ranks for Bryan. Beth tapped me on the arm and asked me who I was looking for. I just looked back at her. She pointed to a soldier right in front of me. "That's Bryan," she said. I had not even recognized my own son. The soldier standing before me was a man I had never seen before. His chiseled, muscular frame filled out his uniform perfectly. My son had become a man and a soldier. But he was wearing those god-awful Army-issue glasses.

After his graduation, Bryan was stationed at Fort Lewis, Washington as part of the 3/2 Stryker Cavalry Regiment, and he was assigned to the 4/2 (Deuce Four) Brigade right before his first deployment to Iraq.

It was in Tacoma that he met his bride-to-be, Tiffany Kasinger. Bryan was almost immediately deployed to Iraq after his assignment to Fort Lewis. My little boy who had climbed trees, played baseball, teased his little sister, broken bones, and drove my old hot rod, was going to war. He didn't know their names, but he was going to do as he promised: avenge the victims of 9/11.

Not long after Bryan was deployed, Tiffany gave us a banner with a blue star on a white field with a red border and trimmed in gold fringe. She told us it represented a family member deployed overseas.

We had no idea there was one of these banners with a Gold Star on it.

Bryan served proudly, and we were always pleased to receive letters, phone calls, emails, and even texts from him. He told us stories of his adventures and about the other soldiers he met along the way.

He was stationed in Mosul, Iraq in December of 2004 when we heard the news that the mess tent at Forward Operating Base (FOB) Marez had been attacked by a suicide bomber. The bomber, fourteen U.S. soldiers, four Iraqi soldiers, and four Haliburton employees were killed in the blast. The entire base went on communication blackout.

At home, we received calls asking about Bryan. We had no news. Tiffany hadn't heard any reports at all. We were desperate for some word, any word.

Bryan called us a few days later. He told us he was okay but that he had to get off the phone quick due to the line of soldiers waiting to get news to their families.

I think that was the biggest sigh of relief I had ever let out.

I knew Bryan was in harm's way. But that thought got shoved to the back of my mind every time I received a phone call or letter from him.

That first year went slowly past, and then Bryan was home. We had just had a new house built, so his Welcome Home Party was in our new home with family, aunts and uncles, grandparents, and friends.

Bryan and Tiffany had been married over the phone on July 10, 2006 while she was on her way to Germany to meet him at the Army Garrison in Grafenwöhr. Their wedding anniversary is one day before ours. Both of our grandchildren, Makya and Zander, were born in Amberg, Germany.

We had the pleasure of flying to Nuremberg where Bryan picked us up in their BMW and drove us along the Autobahn to their cute little house in Vilsek. Makya was less than a year old and so tiny in Bryan's arms. Tiffany would dress her up in a Teddy Bear suit whenever we would go out into the Germany winter.

The German trains have wonderful cars! There was a tiny seat between the table and the window where Tiffany would place Makya for the trip. Makya was completely contented to sit there and just observe everything. Even the conductor commented on how cute she was in her little bear suit.

When Makya was older, we were playing with her and Zander at a playground. Makya ran up to Beth and asked, "Grandma, know what I wish?" Beth thought maybe Makya wished for ice cream, or maybe even a pony since her birthday was coming up, but instead, Makya said, "I wish my daddy hadn't died." Makya kissed Beth and then went right back to playing.

Beth was simply stunned. We all wished Bryan hadn't died, but to hear the words from a seven-year-old was completely surprising and stunning. Makya was old enough when Bryan was killed to remember her daddy playing with her. Zander was so young, he was three years old, and Bryan had been deployed for most holidays and birthdays, so Zander had few memories of his daddy.

Beth wears a dog tag with Bryan's photo on it and Zander will point to it and say, "That's my daddy." So, he knows, but his memories will likely be ours or Makya's.

Chapter 2
There Are No Instructions

Bryan's family and friends sat with us in a waiting room just off the airstrip at Fort Campbell where he was to arrive from Dover AFB. Brigadier General Jeff Colt entered the room and the soldiers in the room snapped to attention. He told the soldiers to be at ease because he was just there to talk to Bryan's family, and to present us with the pin that would designate us as a Gold Star family.

~ The official military pin which designates
an immediate family member of a fallen soldier.

As he pinned one on Zander's shirt, Zander reached out and tapped the star on the General's shoulder as if that was the star he wanted instead. The General told Zander he might have to wait a few years before he received that star.

We would all have rather had that other star.

The jet carrying Bryan arrived and I carried his son, Zander, in my arms out to the tarmac, hoping my legs would be able to carry us both.

There were many different thoughts that went through my head on April 8, 2011 as I looked at my son's flag-draped coffin. Everything from regret to pride played out in my mind. A life taken too soon is tragic enough, but when a parent has to bury their child, well, "tragic" does not even begin to convey that feeling.

"Staff Sergeant Bryan A. Burgess was not only a fine soldier, he was a good friend..." the words being spoken by Sergeant Brent Schneider finally caught my attention. He went on to say how in November of 2010 Bryan and his team had inserted themselves in the line of fire between the Taliban and Schneider's platoon, saving Schneider's, and many others' lives that cold November day. An action that would eventually see Bryan being posthumously awarded the Bronze Star Medal of Valor.

Brent's precious daughter, Ava, took me by the hand later that day and told me that Bryan was her angel because he had saved her daddy from the monsters. I hugged her so tight I think she squeaked. It was just one story of many, many more of Bryan's experiences in the U.S. Army that we would hear in the coming days, months, and years.

My wife, Beth, and I were seated in the front row of the small, white-washed chapel that sat on base at Fort Campbell, Kentucky. With us were Bryan's widow Tiffany, Bryan's mother, Linda, his step-dad, Randy, and his sister, Brandi.

Beth held my hand as I stoically listened to Sergeant Schneider talk about Bryan, his service, and his friendship. Time seemed to be jumping from moment to moment, but at the same time moving in slow-motion.

It's nearly impossible to describe how it felt to have to hold myself still in my chair while a cadre folded Bryan's Flag, snapped the creases, tucked the corners, smoothed the fabric with white-gloved hands; and then to see Brigadier General Jeff Colt kneeling and handing the flag to Tiffany.

> **We had become a Gold Star Family.**

As the service ended, people began filing past Bryan's casket. The casket remained closed. At least, that's the way I remember it. I was impressed, but not totally surprised, by the number of people in attendance, but a sudden BANG from Bryan's casket startled me. A Special Forces Green

Beret was standing at the foot of Bryan's casket. As he turned to leave, another Green Beret stepped forward, placed a pin on Bryan's casket, and brought his fist down with a BANG, driving the pin into the wood.

We learned that Bryan had signed up for the Green Berets. He had already been taking classes and training there on base at Fort Campbell. Tiffany told us that by driving their Special Forces pins into Bryan's casket with their fists, they had accepted him as one of their own.

There were other funerals going on at Fort Campbell that day. Bryan and five other soldiers from Task Force No Slack had been killed in action in Afghanistan on March 29, 2011. Six families had been devastated. In the months and years to come, those other families and the men that had served and fought beside Bryan would become our family.

*****

Bryan Allan Burgess was born on April 23, 1981 to Terry and Linda Burgess in Cleburne, Texas on a very dark and stormy morning. Linda had been in labor with Bryan for almost twenty-four hours. My parents, Chal and Doris, had been caught in the storm on Interstate I-20 on their way to Cleburne from Clyde, and they were stranded out near Eastland. Linda's parents, Jimmy and Joy, were there to hear Bryan enter our world. I remember thinking that I'd never heard a louder, more wonderful sound than that of my new-born son hollering at the top of his lungs.

Bringing a new life into this world is as scary as it is exhilarating. An entire world of possibility opens up for that precious little being taking his first lung-full of air. I wanted him to surpass me in everything from I.Q. to success in his life. I was holding an extension of two families. Right then, Bryan Allan Burgess was my entire future.

*****

SSG Bryan A. Burgess was cremated per his wishes on April 12, 2011. His sister, Brandi Starr, woke up screaming that morning that she was on fire. They were 800 miles apart.

Bryan and Brandi had been closer as siblings than I had ever been with either of my two brothers. My children were the quintessential big brother and little sister. As they grew older they, of course, had gone different paths and had their own friends, but they still shared that bond and that closeness of spirit that transcends any distance.

~ Bryan and Brandi, Arkansas, 1989

~ Bryan and Brandi, 1993

Siblings of deceased brothers and sisters don't have a handbook on how to deal with death and loss.

~ Bryan and Brandi, 2002

Therapy allows the sibling to discuss some of their feelings that they wouldn't otherwise talk about with their parents, but those deepest, darkest thoughts of being abandoned not only by their sibling, but also by their parents, still circulate.

Brandi has honored her big brother in so many different ways, and I'm proud to use her as an example. She and her mother arranged for a memorial bench to be placed for Bryan at Hulen Park in Cleburne. The bench faces the American Flag near the center of the park where we all used to play, have picnics, and celebrate birthdays.

Brandi also started a line of handmade jewelry that she created in memory of Bryan. She even operated her own little shop at a flea market for several years.

Brandi was interviewed by a local magazine, *Burleson NOW*, and a photo of her holding Bryan's portrait graces the cover of the May 2015 issue.

~ *Burleson NOW*, May, 2015

The article focuses on the way Bryan's family all came together to adopt a Texas Highway for the "Don't Mess With Texas" trash pickup campaign.

One of Bryan's pet peeves was people throwing trash out of their car. He loved Texas, and he certainly did not appreciate people "messing with it." It seemed only natural that we should do a small part of keeping it clean for him.

Beth worked tirelessly for over a year with the Texas Department of Transportation to find a highway close to Cleburne that we could adopt as Bryan's family. In September of 2013, a section of highway on FM 917 (Farm to Market Road 917) in Joshua, Texas, became available. In 2017, we were able to move to a different, shorter, and much safer section to clean just north of Crowley, Texas on FM 731.

~ Bryan's Highway Cleanup Sign, May 04, 2015

~ Bryan's Highway Cleanup Volunteers, March 31, 2018

We have never been disappointed when we ask for volunteers to come help us clean up Bryan's highway!

*****

Some of Bryan's ashes are in a little golf bag urn that sits on a shelf in our living room, with the ashes of his grandmother, Doris Burgess. In fact, our living room, as well as the entry hall, has become our shrine to Bryan. Gone are the usual home decorations, and in their place are photos, medals, a beautiful charcoal portrait of Bryan by artist Michael Reagan, and a huge Challenge Coin case. I am not a decorator, so the memorabilia are slightly scattered and not at all coordinated. But were you to point to any one item in that hallway and ask about it, I could tell you stories…

There is a coin from the Patriot Guard Riders (PGR) near the top of our challenge coin case. I knew about the PGR, but April 8, 2011 was my first direct encounter with them. As we were escorted off base from Fort Campbell, I marveled at the endless line of soldiers along either side of the street. Each of them was holding a steady sharp salute as we passed by. As we left Fort Campbell and pulled out onto the highway to Clarksville, hundreds of motorcycles roared into life. American Flags, Unit Flags, POW Flags, Kentucky and Tennessee Flags and even a few Texas Flags were flying behind the Patriot Guard Riders as we were escorted to the Funeral Home in Clarksville. The line of motorcycles stretched beyond sight ahead of us.

The Patriot Guard Riders were already standing "Tall and Silent" as we approached the Funeral Home. I didn't want to go inside. So, I stalled by going to each rider in the flag line, shaking their hand, and thanking them for being there. I remember being moved by their tears.

Beth came outside to find me, and she took my hand as we entered the Funeral Home together. Bryan's casket was behind a closed door and we stood restlessly in the hallway as friends and family gathered, shook our hand, patted us on the shoulder, mumbled condolences and then shuffled off.

During my last visit with Bryan and Tiffany at Fort Campbell, I had bought a commemorative knife. I had brought the empty knife case with me and I set it out on the guest register podium for Bryan's men to autograph.

By the end of the day, autographs covered the case, even one from Brigadier General Colt and Colonel Joel "JB" Vowel.

At the other end of the funeral home, a local family was gathered for a loved one. They were all in casual clothes and here we all were in suits, dresses, and military dress uniforms. I remember catching the eye of one of the family, and they gently placed their right hand over their heart and slowly nodded at me. I turned to fully face them and gave them a nod of my head. My attention was taken by Tiffany as she took my hand and asked me, "Are you ready?"

I thought I was.

There are no instructions on how to handle an untimely death. There is no manual on this planet that can prepare you for the shock and trauma of hearing that your child has been killed on foreign soil. The Armed Forces does not present the parents of a new recruit with a worst-case scenario handbook.

The sense of pride at what Bryan had accomplished in his lifetime and during his military career had not yet descended on me. Right then I was simply a father grieving for his son.

> There are no instructions on how to handle an untimely death. There is no manual on this planet that can prepare you for the shock and trauma of hearing that your child has been killed on foreign soil.

As the Honor Guard opened the door to Bryan's room, I felt the blood drain from my head. My feet simply refused to move. Everyone in the hallway was waiting for me to go into the room first. Beth gently took my other hand in hers, I took a deep breath, and the three of us apprehensively walked into the room.

Two members of the Fort Campbell Honor Guard stood at either end of Bryan's casket, which was open and gently lit by soft lamps from above. I think I focused on every detail in that room except Bryan. When my eyes focused on my boy's face...

You've seen those movie shots where the main character comes into sharp focus and the rest of the room seems to grow rapidly around them? That actually happens. All the air left me in a vacuum. There was no light but the light on Bryan's face. There was absolutely no sound.

I reached out and touched Bryan's white-gloved hands; hands that would never again hold his children, hands that would never again caress his wife's face, hands that would never again embrace me.

One thought pierced through my brain: *How can I possibly live up to my son's sacrifice?*

This is how. By telling Bryan's story. By telling our story of how we live up to his ultimate sacrifice.

Chapter 3
Grief Never Takes a Holiday

Bryan's Birthday

Bryan was killed on March 29, 2011, just sixteen days before his next leave. His birthday is on April 23. Tiffany, along with SFC Lyons and his family, had planned a trip to Disney World for Bryan's birthday and his Welcome Home party.

Instead of a huge birthday celebration for Bryan, we attended his funeral.

Mother's Day

Bryan was deployed on Mother's Day, 2010. It was to be the last one he would ever celebrate with Tiffany.

Special Days

Memorial Day, 2011, and this holiday ever since, have taken on a much darker, brooding meaning for us. It became no longer simply a holiday of decorations we could take down from the closet shelf, dust off, and hang on the front door. Memorial Day became as precious and sacred to us as Bryan's birthday or the day of his death.

Family, friends, and neighbors learned that to say "Happy Memorial Day!" to us was like yanking an adhesive bandage off your arm. There was nothing "Happy" about the day. It is a day to honor every single deceased Veteran and Service Member.

In 2010 the Crowley Veterans Memorial Committee was formed and their mission was to create a plaza that would honor local heroes who have served and are currently serving our nation. The plaza was to be opened and dedicated on Memorial Day, 2015. Two members of the committee, Johnny Shotwell and Christine Gilbreath, invited us to submit Bryan's name and information to be engraved on the Soldier's Cross pedestal that sits in the middle of the plaza's fountain.

On the morning that Bryan's name was to be engraved, the Committee called me and said I would be allowed to take photos of the engraving. I rushed right over there. The young man doing the work had his equipment set up and he was taping up a template with Bryan's name onto the marble slab. I was taking photo after photo and the young man turned to me and asked me if I knew Bryan. I replied that I was his dad. The young man stood, shook my hand, and told me that he had attended school with Bryan.

Small world.

~ Crowley Veteran's Plaza

On the Sunday before Memorial Day, Beth and I meet friends and family at Dallas-Fort Worth (DFW) National Cemetery to place flags at the head stones. After "Taps" is played, we take our bundle of flags and make our way to a row of headstones, saying aloud the name engraved on the headstone, placing the flag, and then moving on to the next headstone.

Beth's father and mother are both buried at DFW National. She and her sisters hold hands and then lovingly place a flag on the grave. It's a sign of respect few Americans witness.

~ Debi, Fran, and Beth at DFW National Cemetery
Memorial Day, 2018

Looking around the cemetery after all the flags have been placed has a profound effect on everyone there. This is the true cost of our freedom.

As for the other holidays during what we now refer to as our "Grief Calendar":

Father's Day just hurts. Knowing I will never again hear my son tell me "Happy Father's Day" brings tears to my eyes. Knowing his children will never be able to hug his neck or fix him a "pasghetti sandwich" just breaks my heart.

July 4th feels just like Memorial Day. Being able to celebrate our freedom comes at a very high cost.

Thanks to Kelly Castonguay of Trophy Club, Texas we have driven the Hornet's Nest Cruiser in their 4th of July Parade twice. Kelly, who is also part of our amazing Snow Ball Express "family", is one of the most patriotic and truly caring people we know.

Our Wedding Anniversary, July 11, is one day after Bryan and Tiffany's.

Labor Day weekend reminds me of all the cookouts I enjoyed with Bryan and of all the cookouts he will now miss with his family.

September 11 is a day of dread.

In 2015, we were invited by Gene Sweeny of Salt of the Earth U.S.A. to tell Bryan's story at the annual ceremony conducted at the 9/11 Fallen Heroes Memorial at Patriot's Park in Venice, Florida. Bryan's name, along with the names of his five fallen brothers of March 29, 2011, was engraved on the base of the memorial which holds a beam from the Twin Towers in New York City. The beam was carried from Ground Zero to Venice, Florida by a truck driven by Carl and Carol Wallin.

Carl and Carol opened their home and hearts to us during our stay in Florida, and they are now part of our "family."

My birthday, November 8, holds no meaning.

Veteran's Day, November 11, allows us to honor the men of No Slack who had returned home.

Thanksgiving? Not even. It's uncomfortable hearing everyone around the table taking turns saying what they're thankful for. I can usually mumble, "Family," and just leave it at that. I spend a lot of holidays saying what I think everyone expects me to say.

Christmas? Being "merry" is just not going to happen.

New Years? Just another year without Bryan in it.

Valentine's Day? A horrible reminder that Bryan's daughter, Makya, will never have a "date" with her daddy.

And then back to March.

Even that first Leap Year after Bryan was killed taunted us with a full year of Twenty-Ninths on the calendar.

It's very, very hard to put the word "Happy" in front of any holiday that we will never again celebrate with Bryan. It was a long time before we stopped feeling guilty about celebrating a holiday without him. We would feel guilty if something made us laugh, or if we enjoyed anything from a good, hot meal to a good, long, hot shower.

Honoring and remembering Bryan is not just one day a year, and it's not just on his birthday or any one particular day. Almost every single day there is a memory revisited that will bring back a happy smile or a tear. It's hard to push through the sad, dark thoughts of a future without Bryan and to remember all of the wonderful, fun times we enjoyed in the past.

Beth wears a dog tag which bears Bryan's photo. Cashiers sometimes notice the dog tag and will casually ask about it. When Beth explained the dog tag to one cashier, the cashier literally backed away from Beth and the counter. Beth quietly said, "It's not contagious."

Other cashiers will ask Beth if they can hold the dog tag. As they gently take the tag in their hands, more times than not, a tear will form in their eyes. Some cashiers are veterans themselves and immediately know what the dog tag symbolizes.

There are people out there who understand not only the sacrifice of a son or daughter, but the sacrifice for their freedom.

> There are people out there who understand not only the
> sacrifice of a son or daughter,
> but the sacrifice for their freedom.

Images of Bryan were constantly in front of me. He was everywhere and in everything. Holidays made me think of special things he had said or done.

Easter, a Holy day, brought one of my most treasured memories to light. I was divorced from Bryan's mother, and he and I were visiting a friend's house for Easter in 1987. There was a large gathering of family there and the Easter egg hunt prize was a huge, cellophane-wrapped basket filled with candy, chocolate, and toys.

Bryan won the prize basket.

I could hear the moms whispering about this stranger who had just waltzed in and taken their kids' prize. But before anyone actually said anything, Bryan stepped forward, tore the wrapping off the basket, stepped *back*, and yelled, "Dig in!" Bryan didn't take a single piece of candy until every other kid there—and some of the moms—had helped themselves. It was one of the first signs I observed that Bryan possessed a rare and special spirit. He was only six years old.

~ Bryan in a tree, age 5, 1986

One of my earliest memories of thinking Bryan just might be interested in the Army was when his grandmother, Doris Burgess, would sing the Vacation Bible School song about being in the Lord's Army:

> I may never march in the infantry,
> Ride in the cavalry,
> Shoot the artillery,
> I may never fly o'er the enemy,
> But I'm in the Lord's Army!

~ Author unknown * Public Domain

Bryan learned that song at age two or three and it was one of his favorites. He and his grandmother would march and ride and fly all over the house singing that song. And in the U.S. Army, Bryan did every one of those things.

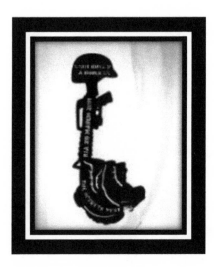

Chapter 4
The Workplace Perspective

I worked for a large financial company for many, many years. While Bryan was home on leave, I was laid off due to that large financial company outsourcing my job to the Philippines.

Beth was in the middle of an important project at work, but she encouraged me to travel to Fort Campbell to be with Bryan on his twenty-ninth birthday.

It was a wonderful week filled with shopping at the huge Opry Mills Mall which had a large, open aquarium filled with stingrays and sharks, eating at Bryan's favorite restaurants, cookouts, bowling, movies, and a birthday party at Dave & Buster's. When I had asked Bryan what he really wanted for his birthday he had at first said he wanted the game "The Beatles: Rock Band," but he knew I was out of a job and he wouldn't let me spend the money on him for something silly. So instead, he picked out a pair of high-quality, Army-authorized utility boots. My very practical son.

It was a wonderful week with my son and his family that I will cherish forever.

Then, just three months later, on Mother's Day, Bryan was deployed to Afghanistan.

So, there I was, unemployed at the same time my son was killed on foreign soil. Being unemployed allowed me time to grieve for my son. Beth, who was employed by the same company, was given the standard corporate policy of three days bereavement leave to grieve for her step-son— the same policy that gives twelve-weeks for the birth of a child.

Three days had elapsed from the time we received the phone call from Tiffany telling us about Bryan being killed in action to the time we were in Dover for Bryan's Dignified Transfer. Three days of grieving had already been spent before we even got to Bryan's funeral at Fort Campbell.

On February 4, 2013 I went back to work for the same company but in a different capacity. I was hired by a supervisor who had been a good friend in the past. The new job entailed a lot of attention to small details. I tried to focus. I really tried, but not to the extent that my supervisor and manager thought I should be exerting myself and directing my efforts.

I was on a conference call and I remember the conversation concerning a detail about whether to use "if" or "is" in a sentence in the customer's statements. The arguments went on for nearly the entire hour of the conference call. I don't know for sure how long the call lasted because I slammed my knee upward into the underside of my desk, yelled that the entire conference call was a totally *bleep* waste of time, and that it didn't matter in the least what the *bleep* statement said because no one ever read the *bleep* statements anyway. I slammed the headset down on my desk and stormed off to the men's room.

A co-worker found me in the men's room and made sure I was okay. He asked me about what happened to set me off. I told him that nothing we, or I, did was of any kind of importance. That everything we did in our department was just a piddling waste of time. It just didn't matter.

He helped me calm down, and then I sheepishly walked back to my desk and apologized to my co-workers.

Soon I was called into the office.

This was all going on at the same time as the promotion of *The Hornet's Nest* movie. Beth and I were deeply involved in the promotion tour, visiting different cities, colleges, and military bases to screen the movie, and in almost every case, talking to the audiences. I was either unaware or just ignoring the toll that was being taken on my heart and soul every time we screened the film.

Beth and I used up our vacation and sick time as fast as it was accrued.

In the office were my supervisor and her boss from New York. Simply put, they said, I was absent a lot, and even when I was in the office I "wasn't there" for my team, and they wanted my assurance that I would put "that nonsense" behind me and be more focused on my work. I could not give them that assurance.

I think they gave me a week to talk it over with Beth and "other parties involved." I talked to Beth that night and she told me what I had been thinking anyway, that Bryan's death and the movie were not in any way, form, or fashion "nonsense."

And so, I was unemployed again for the second time in three years.

We have since found out that approximately 80% of Gold Star dads lose their jobs after the death of their son or daughter. This is by no means a hard fact since no study exists (yet) to determine that figure. By my own reckoning, and due to conversations that I have had with other Gold Star dads, of the 8,000+ combat related deaths from the wars in Iraq and Afghanistan, approximately 6,400 Gold Star dads become unemployed due to the loss of a son or daughter.

The other dads I have spoken with have voiced much the same concerns and issues I experienced in trying to deal with the "real" world after a traumatic death. Living with death is not easy, especially if you are engaged in trying to honor your fallen hero while you are pretending to care about your job. Day-to-day details that used to seem somehow crucial have now become trivial and unimportant.

I am fortunate that Beth helped to support us while we toured with *The Hornet's Nest* movie. Money always gets a little tight, but her support helped us take the movie coast-to-coast and again, in every instance, tell Bryan's story.

Beth's work career revolved around fixing problems with software. Bryan's unexpected death and the heartbreak can never be fixed. Regrets cannot be fixed or re-written. It's a daily, internal struggle we deal with.

To those who think that a career is paramount, Beth puts it like this:

"I was supposed to go to Kentucky for my stepson's birthday shortly before he deployed to Afghanistan with his Army unit. A huge project was coming up at work, so I didn't go. I chose my job over my family. I promised my husband I would be there when Bryan came home at the end of the deployment a year later. I kept that promise, but not in the way I ever imagined as I stood on the tarmac and watched the Honor Guard carry his casket off a plane. I had no idea April 23, 2010 would be his last birthday and he would be KIA (Killed In Action) March 29, 2011. At his funeral I made myself and my husband another promise that I have not broken in the seven years since. I would never choose a job over my family again."

Nobody goes to the grave wishing they'd spent more time at the office.

Beth now works for a financial institution that was created solely to assist service members with their financial needs, especially during a crisis. Her co-workers are mature adults who understand the service and sacrifice service members and their families experience in times of war. The differences between the former workplace and her current one are absolutely astounding.

> Nobody goes to the grave wishing they'd spent more time at the office.

Chapter 5
Triggers and Honors

I was never one to believe in the Pennies from Heaven myth. Until it saved my life.

I had dropped off our FJ Cruiser at Firestone to have the tires rotated and decided to walk over to Big Lots to spend some time. At the edge of the driveway between Firestone and Big Lots was a shiny penny. I stopped and picked up the penny just as a Fed Ex truck sped past my head around a blind corner. The Fed Ex driver was just as startled as I was. Had I not stopped to pick up the penny I would have been hit by the truck. Hard.

The penny's date: 1981. Bryan's birth year. But the penny was as shiny as if it were brand new. It's taped into my journal.

We seem to find more dimes than pennies in our path. Some of the more metaphysical websites will tell you that dimes represent a continuation and the highest integrity. It's easy for me to believe that Bryan puts these symbols in my path.

Another Fed Ex experience was much better. A friend of ours, Cherry, created artificial Fall pumpkins with the No Slack scroll painted on them. Beth ordered one, and she got a call from Cherry saying that she had missed the regular mail so she was sending us the package via Fed Ex instead.

When the package arrived, Beth went out to meet the Fed Ex driver. The driver was Rosa Beard and she was shaking the package as she approached Beth. She asked what was supposed to be in the box because it felt empty. Beth described the pumpkin to her. On our porch is a wreath on a stand that has Bryan's photo on it. As Beth was talking about No Slack, the driver focused on Bryan's photo. Her eyes began filling with tears and she told Beth, "I served with him in Iraq." Small world, indeed. Rosa remains a close friend to this day.

Music, too, plays a huge part in the grief process. From songs that Bryan enjoyed to the music played at his funeral, we have been "triggered" by many of them.

Bryan was designated a special guest of honor at American Airlines Sky Ball XI on October 5, 2013 in Dallas, Texas. The theme of Sky Ball that year was the United States Army, and since American Airlines had worked closely with

The Hornet's Nest movie production, Bryan, a local hero, was going to be featured during the gala.

Brent Dones, one of the producers for *The Hornet's Nest*, and videographer Bob Vincent, both of whom are dear friends and part of our new "family," asked us to send them as many photos of Bryan as we could, anything from baby photos to school portraits to Boot Camp and deployments. All those photos were made into a heartfelt video which played on a four-sided video screen suspended above the crowd of 3,000 attendees in Hanger Five at DFW Airport.

Ron White, the creator of the Afghanistan Memory Wall, was writing—from memory—the names of the 2,300 fallen killed in Afghanistan. As he began writing Bryan's name on the wall, a spotlight illuminated his hand and the entire audience witnessed his pen write Bryan's name on the marble slab.

During Sky Ball, it is natural to hear people talking and walking around, dishes clattering, and chairs scraping the floor. As Ron was writing Bryan's name on that wall, the only sound I could hear was sobbing. It was a very, very special tribute to my son who had become a hero to almost 3,000 people.

It had been a momentous day for us. I had drained my phone's battery with so many photos and video that I couldn't even turn it on. On our way back to the hotel, about

3:00 am, we stepped off the elevator and suddenly we heard the Beatle's *Hard Day's Night* blaring. I told Beth that was some rude behavior playing music that loud that late at night.

Beth pointed at my cell phone and said, "It's coming from your phone." I tried to deny it because my phone battery was dead, but sure enough, the speaker was blaring *Hard Day's Night*. I couldn't even turn down the volume. We got into the room and plugged the phone in and were able to finally get the screen to come on. Beth told me, "It's coming from your Pandora music." I replied, "That's interesting since I don't have Pandora on my phone."

One of Bryan's all-time favorite bands was, you guessed it, The Beatles. We took it as his way of telling us he was proud of what all we had accomplished with *The Hornet's Nest* movie, The Afghanistan Memory Wall, and Sky Ball XI.

*****

Right before we left the house to go to Bryan's funeral service at Fort Campbell, Tiffany took me out to Bryan's truck and told me she wanted me to hear the song that was going to play at Bryan's funeral. Tiffany inserted the CD and the song "If I Die Young" by the Band Perry began playing. It was the perfect song. We were both crying before the first chorus was even finished.

A few months ago, we were in a store and "If I Die Young" started playing over the loudspeakers. We abandoned our shopping cart and just left the store. It's a beautiful, meaningful song, but it holds such a horrible connotation for us now that we can't bear to listen to it. It's very much like "Taps" and "Amazing Grace." Those songs hold nothing but very difficult triggers for us.

On the other hand, the Beatles' music, especially the songs that Sunny Lyons selected for Bryan's memorial service are very soothing. I don't know if it's because those are songs I grew up with or what. I grew up with "Amazing Grace," too.

Every grieving parent will have those types of "triggers" that just set them off. Sometimes even other family members don't realize what those triggers are.

We routinely mailed packages of beef jerky and razors to Bryan in Iraq and Afghanistan. When Beth and I were shopping in Costco she had wandered over to cosmetics and I was in the snack aisle. I spotted the beef jerky I used to send to Bryan and immediately my eyes filled with tears. I turned away to find Beth right behind me, holding a package of the razors we used to mail to him. Her lower lip was quivering. She put the package down and we left the store. Those are triggers.

I wrote this back in 2014 as I was headed home on the Trinity Rail Express:

"There are times when the past rushes in and flows over you like a wave, and the undertow of regret pulls you to a deep place you thought to avoid. That time came today as I was simply walking across a vacant parking lot where a father was walking behind his son as the boy peddled his tiny bike across the asphalt. An un-beckoned flood of memories washed over me. I saw myself standing there as Bryan learned to work the pedals of his first bicycle. All too quickly the years sped past my eyes as I walked across the parking lot.

"I stole one last look at the father and his son, the man's large yet gentle hand on the boys back as he guided him safely along. I hope that I guided Bryan that way. It's too late for regrets. Too late for a last "I'm proud of you." As the wave of memories left me, my eyes were moist, the pavement was a little blurry, but my load seemed lighter. It was as if a strong, yet gentle hand was on my back, guiding me along."

Chapter 6
A Military Death,
A Gold Star Retreat

We hear many Gold Stars say that they want to make sure their son or daughter is never forgotten. They want the memory to live on. We discovered that with a military death, keeping their memory alive is more than possible. There are websites dedicated to fallen heroes, there are memory walls and veteran's plazas and events. There are many organizations dedicated to Gold Star Families. But you have to look for them.

When Beth saw that I was sinking into a depression after all the ceremonies had ended and the cards, letters, and casseroles started tapering off, she found lots of organizations for Gold Star Mothers, Gold Star Widows, and even Gold Star Kids. She found nothing for Gold Star Dads and certainly nothing for Gold Star Parents.

That's why we took it upon ourselves to create Gold Star Parent's Retreat, to include both parents. Even from my generation, dads are expected to be 'stoic' and at times 'emotionally stable.' As hard as it is to let others know my heart is still broken and that there are times I will still sit on my deck and just bawl over my loss, I want dads to know that it is natural and normal to weep when we talk about our sons and daughters. It's a show of love and for most dads those tears are the highest form of respect.

I am very thankful that I married a woman strong enough to carry two broken hearts.

Beth took it upon herself to reach out to other Gold Stars. She joined a group that sent sympathy cards to families of fallen soldiers and she started collecting names of families and soldiers. She got in touch with other Texas Gold Stars and discovered some events organized specifically for honoring fallen heroes.

One of those events was called The Riley Run, in Tolar, Texas. Organized by Mic and JoAnn Stephens, they honor their son, Army Sgt. 1st Class Riley Stephens by holding a 5K run each year in Tolar. Beth found out that Tolar has a population of 885. Tolar has lost two of their own in the wars in Vietnam and Afghanistan.

Mic's son, Ken Stephens, organized a Suck It Up Ruck to honor three fallen soldiers, his brother Riley, SFC William

"Bill" Brown, and Chief Warrant Officer 2, "Big Mike" Duskin.

I had an urge to push myself, almost to the point of penance, so I joined up with the group at the DFW National Cemetery. It was the first time I met Mic Stephens and his family along with David Roberts. Both of them are Gold Star dads and both of them do an exceptional job of honoring their sons. We paused at each of their son's graves and had a toast in honor of them. Mic and Dave added a toast for Bryan. We became family right then and there.

After ten miles out on the ruck I started feeling excessively hot and both my calves started cramping. I made it to the top of a hill where the team was waiting and I started throwing up. I had heat exhaustion. I had been drinking water and Gatorade but hadn't been taking in enough electrolytes to replenish what I had lost.

I wound up in an ER thanks to the two wonderful women supporting the ruck, Wendy and Camyle. I sent Beth a text that said, "I'm down" (or something like that). She left work to come pick me up and I went home, a little crushed that I didn't finish the intended twenty-two miles for that day. The plan was to walk twenty-two miles a day for three days. The twenty-two miles were for the twenty-two Veterans that committed suicide every single day and the three days was for the three heroes we were honoring, SFC Riley Stephens, CW2 Mike Duskin, and SFC Bill Brown.

On the second day of the Suck It Up Ruck, while I was supposed to be recuperating, John Skier, his wife, Lisa, and their daughter, Josephine Riley volunteered to take my place in the ruck. I was so determined to finish the ruck that I broke doctor's orders and completed the ruck with all of them by my side.

~ Josephine, Lisa, and John Skier "Suck It Up Ruck"
August 29, 2015

Walking into Granbury, Texas that final day with a troop of veterans, active duty soldiers, friends and Gold Star families all waving American Flags, cemented my resolve to honor Bryan in any possible way.

Carry The Load is a national relay that crosses the country from the West coast to the East coast and meets in Dallas for a two-day, all night march on Memorial Day. At Carry The Load a couple of years ago I pushed myself to walk the entire twenty hours of the event. I walked all night long, only stopping to use the bathrooms or change socks. A dear friend, Gidget Pacheco, walked with me all night. She told me that she understood my "mission" and that she took it as hers, too. Beth tried to get me to stop about 3 or 4 in the morning, but I couldn't sit still. I had to walk. I had to carry Bryan.

> **I had to carry Bryan.**
> **I had to carry my son.**

At the 2018 Carry The Load event I walked with Kevin Hodes, and I told him about the need I'd felt to punish myself. He asked me how I felt this year. I told him I was at peace. We took our time on the trail, stopping to say "hello" to all the incredible people walking and carrying their own loads.

Beth and I have attended many 5K events, and as of this writing we have participated in the Bataan Memorial Death March at White Sands Missile Range in New Mexico twice and the Marine Corps Marathon in Washington, D.C. once. Each event has led us to more and more connections with Veterans and organizations. It would be so much easier (and cheaper) to sit at home and just wait for some organization to hand us a certificate or send us a photo of some event where Bryan was honored.

I can't wait for someone else to make that happen. Bryan's name is known coast to coast simply because Beth and I put ourselves "out there." We go outside and we talk to people. And now those people know Bryan's story.

We attend an annual event in Hempstead, Texas called The Watermelon Run for the Fallen. It was started to honor one of Hempstead's own, SSG Jeffrey Hartley, the son of the town's chief of police. Hartley was killed in April of 2008. The event has become a huge success in honoring all of the fallen soldiers from Texas. Near the end of the event, dozens of citizens, veterans, and active duty servicemen and women line up with their list of the names of fallen warriors for a "Roll Call."

Beth told me that she waits, secretly hoping they won't say Bryan's name, that this has all been a dream. As Bryan's name is said aloud, we hold each other tight, wipe away our tears, and continue listening to the much-too-long list of names.

Beth and I do all of these things in honor of Bryan. We do them despite feeling "old and tired." We do these things because Bryan is not here to do them himself.

A very good friend of ours, Warren Williamson, conducts an annual Tribute to Fallen Soldiers with a cross country motorcycle ride from Oregon to Washington, D.C. Warren drives a motor-home which tows a torch that burns the entire trip. In August of 2017, Warren invited us to meet him and his entourage in Washington D.C. to lay a Gold Star wreath at the Tomb of the Unknown Soldier in Arlington National Cemetery.

I've walked hundreds — if not thousands — of miles, but walking out to the Tomb with Warren and the Old Guard was probably the longest, hardest, and most meaningful walk of my life. If not for me knowing that Bryan was watching, I would not have had the strength.

We sometimes hear about friends meeting strangers who also know us. They start their conversations with their "Burgess story." It makes me smile to think that friends and strangers are making a connection simply because we have shared Bryan's story with each of them.

The morning Bryan was killed and our families started gathering at our house, Beth's cousin, Shandra Dalke, brought me one of the most memorable and unique gifts we have received, a pair of Hulk Hands. They're huge, green, foam filled fists that make Hulk-sounds when you smash with them. Shandra knew anger was one of the first symptoms of grief, and as Bruce Banner says, "You won't like me when I'm angry." The fact that Bryan was a huge

Hulk fan and that I truly just wanted to smash things made those hands a perfect gift on an otherwise horrible day. I still have (and use) those Hulk hands.

Anger and punishment have been constant companions since Bryan was killed. My trigger was very easy to pull. I snapped at something Beth said a couple of times, one time punching a hole through the wall and the next violently sweeping the dinner dishes off the kitchen table crashing to the floor.

After I had calmed down, Beth asked me, "Feel better now?" Embarrassed at my outburst, but feeling truthful, I sheepishly replied, "Yes."

We conducted a "Plate Breaking" therapy session at one of our Gold Star Parents Retreats. We asked the parents to write something they needed to let go of on the plate; like regret, hate, etc. Then we had the parents smash the plates. I still get comments about how much the parents reflect on that session. I gathered all the broken pieces of those plates, gave them to an artist and she created a beautiful soldiers cross mosaic of the broken pieces.

I was having a bad morning recently, trying to deal with my debit card being blocked at a gas station and having to call the bank three times just to find out it was a gas station's faulty card reader that had caused my card to be declined and subsequently blocked for eighteen hours right before we were to go on a six-hour trip to south Texas. This was definitely an issue I was not used to dealing with. I was angry, and my anger was compounded each time I had to call our bank.

When I finally got home, I went into our back yard, our "little oasis," and was watering Beth's plants. A cardinal landed on our back fence and just sat there looking at me. As I was looking at the cardinal, a large, beautiful, green and black dragonfly landed on my right hand. Both of these creatures can represent spirit animals, or totems, and they both have come to represent to me a spiritual presence of either Bryan or my mother giving me a sense of comfort.

As that sense of comfort descended over me and the dragonfly and the cardinal flew away, I could feel my pulse slowing and the anger of the morning's dealings with the bank and the gas stations draining away.

Anger is a very real issue when one is dealing with overwhelming grief. A lot more than just dinner dishes will suffer from anger issues if the anger is not addressed. If not confronted, it has the power to consume you.

We've seen what anger can do to a family that has suffered a tragic loss. There are some cases where husband and wife blame each other for the events that led up to their son's or daughter's death. This is especially true of broken homes.

Even though Bryan came from a broken home, I'm very proud of the fact that my ex-wife and her husband attend our Gold Star Parent's Retreats. We all understand that it is no longer about us, but everything we do now is about Bryan.

If you are dealing with unresolved anger issues, please talk to someone about them. Goodwill Industries has some pretty cheap ceramic plates. Just saying.

"Release"
~ A Mosaic by Kathy Dunn
http://katsuzstore.webs.com

That's what we have to do. Take the shattered pieces of the most horrible day of our lives and try to create something meaningful and whole with them. It's not easy to do. A fragmented life is difficult to live at best, and on the really bad days a fragmented heart simply refuses to beat.

> Take the shattered pieces of the most horrible day of our lives and try to create something meaningful and whole with them. It's not easy to do. A fragmented life is difficult to live at best, and on the really bad days a fragmented heart simply refuses to beat.

We hand out painted rocks at our retreats that simply have one word on them: **Breathe**.

> **Breathe.**

Just like the day I had to make my legs carry me into the room where Bryan lay at rest, I had to force myself to breathe. Ordinary reflexes no longer respond. Our hearts beat, but the blood seems like it is too thick to flow. Our lungs inflate but the air feels like it is too thin. Colors are too bright and sound is too dim. The simple task of getting out of bed and facing another day is almost too daunting. Getting dressed and facing people in social situations made me break out in a cold sweat. Eating was a chore. Chores were often ignored.

Remember when I thought to myself: *"how can I possibly live up to Bryan's sacrifice?"*

That thought still haunts me. I end each day asking myself, "Would Bryan be proud of me today?" That was why I was pushing myself. That was why I felt a need for penance. That was why I had nightmares about Bryan.

Does it matter?

You bet your ass it matters.

Grief Brain

Some people call it "Grief brain." I don't disagree. During 2011, the weeks involved a lot of travel back and forth to Fort Campbell. Tiffany and the kids still lived on base, so we had a place to stay, but the *order* of the events has become jumbled in my mind. I honestly can't remember if the Eagle Remembrance Ceremony happened first or if the Bastogne Memorial was first and I certainly can't separate out who we met where.

I think the Eagle Remembrance Ceremony was first. Eighteen of No Slack's unit had been killed in that last deployment. Bryan's photo was on an easel along with seventeen other photos. There were hundreds of people gathered; military and civilian. It was a breezeless day. No Slack stood in formation behind the podium and the eighteen photos. Even from a distance, I could see tear-streaked faces in the ranks.

The photos and the Bastogne Unit symbol gave me an idea — one of the first on how to honor Bryan. At a dinner on base, one of the soldiers who had served with Bryan told us he loved to play poker with Sgt. Burgess because Bryan sucked at it. I ordered a hundred little photos of Bryan printed on stickers which I attached to poker chips. So, when it came time for us to attend the Bastogne Memorial, I carried those poker chips. I told our escort, Lt. Jacob Sass, that I wanted to meet some of the guys who served with Bryan. He told me, "Good. They want to shake your hand." When we walked around the corner, there were probably eighty No Slack soldiers standing there. With each handshake, I transferred a poker chip. Some of those guys are *still* carrying the Sgt. Burgess Poker Chips.

~ Sgt. Burgess Poker Chips
Photo of Sgt. Bryan Burgess courtesy of Sgt. Nate Allen

When the sympathy cards, letters, and casseroles from well-meaning neighbors and friends *stop* coming, the feeling is almost as bad as when they started. Our mailbox had been filled daily with condolences from family and friends, co-workers, and organizations. It actually hurt when the mailbox contained only bills and junk mail. Neighbors had brought plants, peace lilies, roses, etc., and when that first peace lily died, Beth cried. Now, she almost never sends living plants or flowers to a grieving family.

> When the sympathy cards, letters, and casseroles from well-meaning neighbors and friends *stop* coming, the feeling is almost as bad as when they started.

Losing anything, whether it be a plant, a pet, or even breaking a favorite cup or dish, especially if the object or pet had a connection to the person that is now gone, can be one of those terrible "triggers" that shoots emotions into high gear. It is one more thread unraveled from that silver cord holding our hearts together.

Right before we got home from Bryan's funeral, my mom called me and told me Uncle Bobby had passed away. Uncle Bob was the last of mom's three brothers. He was also one of my most favorite uncles. We had spent many, many summers together at my grandmother's house in Frederick, Oklahoma. Uncle Bobby with his ginormous glass of iced tea and his Mad Magazines stacked in his room. We spent one whole day counting tornado funnels forming over Frederick while granny hollered from the storm cellar that she "wasn't going to watch if we got sucked off God's green earth!"

My brother, Lynn, went with me to Bobby's funeral. I can't remember why mom didn't go. I think it was because she was becoming too ill to travel. Beth had assured me that no one would blame me if I didn't go to his funeral. I told her it was something I had to do or I would later regret it.

Uncle Bob had served in the U.S. Army after Korea. Mom has photos of him in uniform astride a military motorcycle at Gibraltar. An American flag draped Uncle Bob's casket. The service was in a huge tent at graveside there in Frederick. I thought I could handle it. I couldn't. I had to step out. As soon as the first note of "Taps" sounded I covered my ears. I apologized to Lynn as soon as the service was over. We said our goodbyes to the family and headed back to Fort Worth.

 Mom passed away at 5:00 a.m. on December 21, 2012 at her home in Clyde, Texas.

As I tenderly closed her eyelids, I felt like death was the only thing life now held for me.

*****

At Fisher House in Dover, Tiffany had read us Bryan's will, which consisted of a giant blue binder that contained his final decisions in case of, well, you know. Tiffany looked at me and said, "Dad, Bryan left his motorcycle to you." I was so absolutely stunned, delighted, and overwhelmed at the thought that I could only nod my head.

Bryan bought the bike in Fort Worth with the bonus he received in 2005 when he re-upped. It's a 2005 Yamaha V Star Classic 650, a good beginner's bike. His pride and joy, and he had left it to me. Bryan had hauled his bike from Fort Worth to Fort Lewis in Washington to Grafenwohr, Germany and back to Fort Campbell, Kentucky. It only had a little over 3,000 miles on it as of 2011.

Bryan had called me not long after he and Tiffany were stationed in Germany and he told me he was having trouble keeping up with the guys that rode Harleys. He said he got left behind when they were riding up mountains. I could hear the frustration in his voice and I knew his desire to not only "keep up" but to "surpass" was eating at him. I encouraged him to try downshifting as he approached the base of the mountain and to push the bike to redline before shifting. I knew the bike could take it and I knew Bryan could, too. He called me a week later and with a lot of pride in his voice told me, "I beat the Harleys to the top of the mountain!" I was as proud of that as he was!

*****

Even before Beth and I could really catch our breath, we and our families were invited to a special session of the Texas Senate and House on Saturday, May 28th, 2011. As part of the Memorial Day commemoration in Austin, the Senate and House held a joint session to honor fallen heroes of Texas from the previous two years. Present were Governor Rick Perry, President Pro Tempore of the Senate, Senator Steve Ogden (ironically from Bryan, Texas), and Speaker Joe Straus, along with Senator Brian Birdwell, who is now a personal friend, and Representative Berman, each a career military officer from their respective Chamber.

As the name of each fallen hero was called, a family member would walk to the front of the room, meet Governor Perry, and then be presented a Texas State flag from their Representative.

When Bryan's name was called I walked over to Governor Perry and he grasped my hand. I expected a simple handshake, but Gov. Perry held my hand as he asked me several questions about Bryan. How old he was, was he married, did he have kids, where did he grow up and such. I was really unprepared for such a meaningful conversation with such a powerful state official in such a prestigious situation. I'm sure I stuttered out the answers to his questions.

I was guided over to our State Representatives, Wendy Davis and Leticia Van de Putte, who presented me with a Texas flag and a very emotional hug.

The day was so very meaningful and special to all of us. Hearing over ninety names called that morning was one of the first times we realized the enormity of being a Gold Star parent.

In May of that same year Beth and I were invited to attend the Eagle Remembrance Ceremony at Fort Campbell. I rented a trailer and we planned to drive from Fort Worth to Kentucky to pick up the bike and bring it home. The weather had different plans. The day before our trip, monsoon-like rains flooded the mighty Mississippi effectively shutting down all the highways between us and Tiffany. We had to ditch our plan to drive and instead flew to Fort Campbell.

The Eagle Remembrance Ceremony is held monthly at Fort Campbell, Kentucky to honor fallen soldiers deployed in support of Operations New Dawn and Enduring Freedom. Eighteen soldiers were being honored on May 13 of 2011.

After the ceremony we were invited to the General's office for a meeting. Our escort for the day, Lieutenant Jacob Sass, seemed nervous about the meeting as did most everyone else who had been invited. Beth and I put on our most distinguished behavior as we walked the hallway in the Headquarters towards the General's office. Aides, Majors, and Colonels stood at attention as we made our way down the hallway. A colonel knocked on the door and we all held our breath as it slowly swung open.

We were greeted with, "Terry! Beth! Tiffany! How wonderful to see you again!" It was Brigadier General Jeff Colt with his arms spread wide inviting us into his office! A huge collective sigh of relief was released from each one of us.

During the meeting General Colt asked us how our experience with the Army had been after Bryan's death and if there was anything he could do to help. Tiffany immediately told the General that we needed to get Bryan's bike shipped to Texas. General Colt looked at his aide and said, "Make it happen."

Four days later, Bryan's bike was being unloaded from a shipping truck onto my driveway. I'm fairly certain the truck driver had never seen such a myriad of emotional expressions on a person as he saw on me that day. I smiled, I cried, I laughed, and I hugged that bike as if it were Bryan himself.

After taking possession of Bryan's bike, my family asked me if I was going to sell it since I didn't ride. My response was that even if I had to mount it over my fireplace I was never going to sell it. Beth encouraged me to take a motorcycle safety class and before long I had my motorcycle license.

We had met some Patriot Guard Riders and one of them, Jon "Weasel" Meleshenko became a close friend. He encouraged me to join the PGR. My goal at the time was to ride Bryan's bike on a PGR mission, to kind of bring it "full circle."

My very first Patriot Guard Mission was on January 29, 2015 at the John C. Collier Home in Mansfield, Texas for a WWII Army veteran, John S. Hart. My mentors, who became close friends and part of our "new" family, were Randy and Niki Smith. Randy quickly taught me the "ropes" and I proudly stood in my first "flag line."

As the Hart family left the funeral home chapel, they stopped and shook hands with some of the PGR. One woman stopped right in front of me, took my right hand, and said, "Thank you for doing this for us." As tears filled my eyes (and as Rick Crabb says, "That's why we all wear sunglasses!"), my mind flashed back to the funeral home in Clarksville, Tennessee where I had shaken the hands of the PGR and told them, "Thank you for doing this for us."

Full circle indeed.

~ Author with Hugh Garland, 2nd BN 501st 2nd Brigade Geronimo
April 21, 2015

And speaking of circles; there is a photo of a soldier and her military working dog during the end credits of *The Hornet's Nest*. That is Stephanie Durazo and her dog, Rico. Stephanie and Rico were separated at the end of their tour. Rico stayed overseas and Stephanie came home to the U.S.

Rick Crabb called me and asked me if I knew of a dog named Rico that had been in a movie. I laughed and told him yes and asked him why. Rick's son, in Italy, had just adopted Rico and was bringing him home to San Antonio where Stephanie was residing at the time. A mighty emotional reunion took place.

I attended several PGR missions at Dallas-Fort Worth National Cemetery and some surrounding cities. It didn't take me long to figure out I was having difficulty handling the missions. I wanted to stand "tall and silent" like the PGR had at Bryan's funeral. I was even asked to conduct the eulogy at a service at DFW National for a Veteran. With apologies to the North Texas PGR, I hung up my vest. We're still friends with so many of the PGR here in Texas. They are family. The service they provide is priceless. Their respect is immeasurable.

I still ride Bryan's bike.

~ Crowley Veteran's Plaza
Photo used by permission of Jon Meleshenko

Chapter 7
The Hornet's Nest

About six months after I had the dream about Bryan, Beth received a phone call from Chaplin Justin Roberts that served with No Slack on Operation Strong Eagle III. He told her a movie producer was collecting video of Bryan for a documentary film and Justin wanted our permission to send his footage to them. We agreed.

We got more phone calls about the film, about the progress, the setbacks, and then one of the producers, David Salzberg, Jr. called us and asked if we could meet him in Dallas to view the "rough cut" DVD of the film, now being called *The Hornet's Nest*. He told us he had invited Linda (Bryan's mom), her husband Randy, and also Bryan's sister, Brandi, to come see the film. I had sunk into a depression during the last few months, so Beth did her best to get me cleaned up, dressed, and we made our way to the Palomar Hotel in Dallas to meet David.

David Salzberg, Jr. is a true dynamo. He is passionate and driven. He was not at all who I had envisioned. The six of us went up to David's room, he told us a bit about the film, how long it was, how it was segmented, and then he left the room to allow us to watch the film.

We were stunned. I was stunned. There was Bryan, in his full battle gear, on a movie screen. It was a good thing Beth and I were sitting on the bed because I honestly thought I was going to pass out. My haunting dream of Bryan on the morning of March 29 was playing out all over again. As I watched my son through a haze of tears, the meaning of the dream, and the certainty of how I could "salute" him back, filled me with an incredible sense of purpose.

I knew right then that I was to not just mourn the loss of my little boy. That innocent little boy had died when Bryan became a soldier. He wanted me to salute the soldier he had become, to celebrate his life, and to understand the cost of my freedom.

> He wanted me to salute the soldier he had become,
> to celebrate his life, and to understand
> the cost of my freedom.

On the screen Bryan was talking about his kids, saying their names and saying how much he missed them. And then there was the Roll Call. I had never witnessed one.

There was Bryan's Command Sergeant Major standing at attention in front of the entire No Slack Battalion, calling out the names of the fallen. When he said Bryan's name, every one of us heaved a sob. There on the screen and standing at attention were the men we had met months earlier at the Eagle Remembrance Ceremony and the Bastogne Memorial at Fort Campbell. Some were sitting, some were standing, and almost all of them were crying at the service held at Bagram in Afghanistan. Some of the soldiers were kneeling in front of the six Soldier's Crosses on display at the front of the tent. Piled on the crosses were packages of cigarettes, Red Bull cans, packages of candy, Unit patches, name tapes, playing cards, almost anything and everything that had been special to these six soldiers which now symbolized their sacrifice. I was not at all surprised to see a playing card stuck on Bryan's helmet.

There is a very iconic photo of Doc Jacobs kissing Bryan's helmet at the Bagram Ceremony. Doc told me Bryan would kiss their helmets before going out on a mission. Bryan had seen this done in the movie *Cool Runnings* and he did it for his men. Doc simply wanted to pay back the gesture. The image is still so very meaningful to us.

~ Doc Jacobs kissing Bryan's helmet at the Bagram Ceremony
Photo courtesy of SSG Mark Burrell

When I found out that *The Hornet's Nest* movie was going to premier in Dallas in May of 2014, we had our Toyota FJ Cruiser wrapped with the official movie poster, the names of the six soldiers killed, Bryan's portrait, and a U.S. Flag background. Our dear friend, Penny Belcourt, created the design and Blue Skies Graphics in Richland Hills, Texas, applied the wrap. The names of the six soldiers are printed on dog tags displayed on the hood of the FJ Cruiser. Penny called us the day the wrap was being finished and told us we really needed to come to the shop to witness it.

We arrived at the shop and Penny took us into the work area. She told us that normally when the guys were doing a wrap, they listened to loud music, smoked, talked, and joked with each other. The scene before us was one of complete respect. There was no loud music. There was no joking going on. We could have been in a church building for all we knew.

Penny looked at us and smiled. We smiled back. These guys "got it." They understood what this wrapped vehicle now represented.

When we stop at gas stations, grocery stores, restaurants, and even rest areas, there will more than likely be someone waiting for us to ask us about *The Hornet's Nest* movie, tell us they've seen the movie or that they, too, served.

~ Toyota FJ Cruiser featuring *The Hornet's Nest*

Before we got the truck to Dallas for the premier, the producers of *The Hornet's Nest* movie called me and asked if they could borrow the truck. They had seen photos of it on Facebook and wanted the film makers, Mike and Carlos Boettcher to drive the truck on a six-week, fourteen-city tour across the country.

How could I say "no" to that?

Beth and I met Mike and Carlos at their house in Oklahoma City, traded vehicles, and watched them drive off on their tour. It's pretty cool just being acquainted with Mike, Carlos, and their family, but knowing that they were going to be driving our truck, showing the film, and talking about Bryan was very satisfying and comforting to us.

The Dallas premier of *The Hornet's Nest* went very well, with many of our friends and family attending along with many of the No Slack soldiers who were in the film. Wynonna Judd and her husband, Cactus, performed an outdoor concert during the premier, playing the song they had written for the movie's soundtrack.

Beth and I held a screening of *The Hornet's Nest* in Abilene, Texas, and we attended a screening in Oklahoma City with Mike and Carlos. Some of Beth's family drove up from Fort Worth to see the movie.

The next day, Beth's sister called and said that their trip home from Oklahoma City had been very unusual. Normally, there would have been talking, chatting, cutting up, and so on, but instead they drove all the way home in silence. "Stunned silence" is what they said. Beth's sister asked her, "How do you and Terry show and watch that over and over and over? Why do you torture yourselves like that?"

The answer to that question is the same answer to the question I asked myself as I looked at Bryan in his flag-draped casket: *"how can I possibly live up to my son's sacrifice?"*

The Hornet's Nest movie provided a way for me to honor Bryan. It provided a way for me to tell his story to so many people who would have never known him otherwise. The movie is also a true legacy for Bryan's children. Makya and Zander were ages four and three when Bryan was killed. Now they will be able to see their Daddy, hear him saying their names, see what he did and why he died.

When you watch the film, you will hear a song playing throughout most of the footage of No Slack during Operation Strong Eagle III and the entire song plays during the film's closing credits. That song, "Chariots," was written in honor of Bryan's last words as he rested in the arms of medic Eric Matheson. Eric says that Bryan looked skyward and asked, "Where's my chariot?" Eric does not know if

Bryan was simply asking about the MEDIVAC or if maybe there was a deeper, spiritual meaning to Bryan's question.

Matthew Greene and Michael Trella wrote "Chariots" after seeing that segment in *The Hornet's Nest*. It's a haunting song with an incredible amount of feeling behind it.

Beth and I attended the G.I. Film Festival in Washington, D.C. where *The Hornet's Nest* made its film debut. At the after party, the band *Politiks* performed "Chariots."

Beth and I were standing there in front of the crowd, holding hands and crying at the song, and someone came up to Beth, put their arm around her shoulders and whispered to her, "We're always praying for you and Terry." Beth looked up to see Wynonna Judd hugging her.

Wynonna and her husband, Cactus, also wrote a song for *The Hornet's Nest* soundtrack, called "Follow Me." In the film you will see Captain Kevin Mott rounding up a rescue team, and he points to several soldiers and commands, "Follow me!" It's a powerful image as the men of No Slack run through a hail of bullets to attempt the rescue of one of their own.

Meeting Wynonna and Cactus was indeed a highlight of the trip, but hearing Bryan's last words immortalized in a song, especially knowing how much Bryan loved music, is a treasure we will hold in our hearts forever.

*****

As I'm writing this, we are preparing to attend a retirement ceremony for a soldier who Bryan met in Afghanistan. Blair Anderson met Bryan on a mountaintop right before Operation Strong Eagle III. As you read in his Foreword, Blair said he and Bryan talked for less than fifteen minutes. Seven years later, Blair recalls that conversation vividly. And his story was one of many we would hear about Bryan.

One of the men we talked with at the Bastogne Memorial at Fort Campbell told us of the day he and Bryan met. He told us he was carrying a box of supplies past the football field and he saw this other soldier running down the length of the field. The soldier touched the goal post, turned, and ran back the entire length of the field to touch the other goal post, again turning and running the length of the field.

The guy with the box of supplies said he was amazed at the stamina of the runner, but his surprise doubled when, after delivering the box of supplies, he saw the soldier still running on the field. He told himself, "I've got to meet this guy!" The running soldier, of course, was Bryan.

The guy telling us the story said he remembered Bryan being out of breath and simply saying one word, "Push."

I think of that story whenever I feel like just giving up. When I think that I'm not making a difference, or worry that I've done all I can, I "push." That thought of Bryan saying "Push" has helped us do everything from attending his funeral, to promoting *The Hornet's Nest*, to creating our own non-profit organization, to running marathons.

Chapter 8
Fear of the Hereafter

For a couple of months early in 2018 I was experiencing some horrible, horrible nightmares about Bryan. I would see him in the dream and he would be standing beside my bed, his eyes completely blacked out, or sometimes his eyes would appear as deep, empty, black sockets, and he would have a terrible expression of anger or hate on his face. I would wake up screaming or be thrashing in my sleep and Beth would have to fully wake me up.

We discussed the nightmares but couldn't seem to find a way to stop them. And then one morning I saw a notification where one of our Gold Star dads had passed away. His wife stated that he was now reunited and face-to-face with his son.

That statement slapped me in the face. I was afraid to face Bryan. I was afraid he would be ashamed of me, or angry with me for not being there as a dad as he grew up. I feared he would be angry with me for not showing more interest in his military career and personal life. I was afraid to meet him in the afterlife.

I talked to Beth about those feelings. She took me by the hand and we walked into our hallway where the walls are covered with photos, posters, shadowboxes, military challenge coins, and other memorabilia we have collected since Bryan's death. Every single item she pointed to had a unique story, how it related to Bryan either before his death, or how it honored him because of his death. She asked me how I could possibly think that Bryan was not proud of me. She showed me hundreds of social media posts about Bryan, not just from us, but from his No Slack brothers and other friends that we have made over the years.

I slept soundly that night and have not had the nightmare again. The dream I had of Bryan the very morning he was killed assured me that our spirit, or whatever energy we consist of or possess, exists beyond the physical realm.

I know for certain that I will see Bryan again, and I am no longer afraid of what that meeting will bring.

> I know for certain that I will see Bryan again, and I am no longer afraid of what that meeting will bring.

Overcoming fear may never be easy. You and I can find all kinds of posters and banners and even coffee mugs encouraging us to "face our fears." Actually doing it, however, requires more courage than just raising a cup of coffee to our lips.

Bryan wanted to be a U.S. Army Ranger. His long-term goal was to be a member of Special Forces. He was well on his way to achieving his goal. He was signed up for Airborne School which included Ground Week, Tower Week, and finally Jump Week which requires the candidate to complete five jumps at 1,250 feet.

Since Bryan's life was cut short, Brandi and I have faced our fears and literally "jumped" in for him. Brandi skydived on her birthday in 2017 and I have skydived twice for Bryan. The fear of jumping out of an airplane was not really as bad as it sounded since they were tandem jumps and the instructor really did all the work. All I had to do was let him push me out of the plane. Sometimes our circumstances serve to push us to an unknown, but in the end, it can be radically important and good.

> Sometimes our circumstances serve to push us to an unknown, but in the end, it can be radically important and good.

Bryan and I loved watching movies and we especially loved watching movies together. The last movie he and I watched was *Smokey and the Bandit*, a cheesy film about a runner and his bootleg friend making a run across the south to deliver beer.

Had I known that was to be the last movie we shared together, I might have chosen a little more meaningful film. But that's what we've learned. You never know when the last time might be.

> You never know when the last time might be.

After *The Hornet's Nest* movie had been out for a while, we received a message via social media which accused us of "taking all the glory from Bryan's death." The message indicated that we were hoarding recognition and not sharing it with the rest of Bryan's family.

That accusation really hurt us.

We felt like we were simply honoring Bryan and his sacrifice by telling his story to as many people as we possibly could. We had no sense of "glory" in Bryan's death, and we were attending public events that were open to any family member or friend of the family. Our accusers were doing absolutely nothing to honor Bryan.

We stopped in our tracks as we examined everything we had done up to that point in Bryan's memory. We had attended screenings of the film, talked about Bryan, traveled to different cities and towns to speak to various audiences, created a memorial coin for Bryan and given away hundreds of them. We had simply done things that would honor Bryan.

We received an invitation to attend a Dallas Cowboys football game with access to Roger Staubach's suite. There were other distinguished guests invited, among them Captain Tye Reedy and his wife, Alex, some of *The Hornet's Nest* movie crew, and Roger's family. Beth and I enjoyed talking to Roger, telling him Bryan's story, getting autographs on some Dallas Cowboys memorabilia and enjoying some of the game.

The day was memorable, but we were again accused of enjoying an event that some of our family had only dreamed of since they were old enough to become Dallas Cowboys fans. Our reply was, "Which one of your children would you sacrifice to be able to go to a football game? Because that's how we got there."

We have even been accused of making a lot of money from Bryan's death. When we replied that Bryan's widow and children were the ones that received the insurance payment, our accusers mentioned all the profits we made from *The Hornet's Nest* movie.

That statement elicited a laugh from us. We never made a dime from the movie. The movie itself was produced and edited by some wonderful people who had volunteered their nights and weekends to create the film. One of the producers told us that the entire budget for *The Hornet's Nest* movie was about equal to the catering budget for another block-buster film about a survivor in Afghanistan which came out at the same time.

The fear of what other people, even family and friends may think or accuse us of doing to get glory or recognition from my son's death is very real. But the fear of Bryan's sacrifice being ignored is even greater.

> The fear of what other people, even family and friends may think or accuse us of doing to get glory or recognition from my son's death is very real. But the fear of Bryan's sacrifice being ignored is even greater.

We certainly don't drive *The Hornet's Nest* Cruiser to keep a low profile, but when we're driving the FJ Cruiser and a stranger gives us a thumbs-up or a salute, I never think that the gesture is aimed at me. The salute is to Bryan.

> The salute is to Bryan.

Hopefully, the person has seen the movie or at least knows about it and that their recognition is of Bryan's sacrifice. That's all the glory I'll ever need.

Chapter 9
Family Is Not Always By Blood

Beth and I were invited by *The Hornet's Nest* production crew to attend a special screening onboard the *USS Intrepid* in New York City benefiting Easter Seals and The Dixon Center.

After the screening, the crew was going to a dinner for a little more intimate get together. It had been a rainy evening but the skies cleared long enough for us to walk over to the restaurant where everyone was gathering.

It was late in the evening, midnight or so, when we got to the restaurant, so we weren't really paying attention to *where* we were. Christian and David had a table at the back of the restaurant so we walked back there, finally noticing the only women in the place were the ones that were with us. Beth excused herself to go to the restroom and immediately came back and told me there was only one restroom. It dawned on us that we were in a bar that catered to men of an openly alternative lifestyle.

We were all seated around the table and I see this guy walk in whom I had seen at the screening. The guy was scowling and the young woman who was with him had a beaming smile. He was Lee Shaw and his companion was singing artist, Annika Horne. Annika had recorded a song, "Little Soldier."

Lee was working with David and Christian to get it onto *The Hornet's Nest* soundtrack and Lee hadn't made much headway toward his goal. He was about ready to pack up and head back home.

Lee and Annika were introduced to everyone and when we spoke with him we found out we were almost neighbors with Lee back in Texas. We had traveled fifteen hundred miles to meet someone that lived less than ten miles from us. Lee tells the story to this day that we met each other in a bar in New York City.

After hearing Lee and Annika's story, Captain Reedy asked to hear the song. Lee pulled out his cell phone to play the recording and saw that his phone battery was all but depleted. Lee pressed the Play button and miraculously, the entire song played.

When Captain Tye Reedy heard "Little Soldier", he told Lee, David, and Christian that the song was meant to be for Bryan. They heartily agreed.

A few months later, production began on a music video for "Little Soldier." It's a powerful visual that compliments the song in every way. When Lee presented us with the "Little Soldier" CD, he showed us the introduction that Capt. Reedy had written:

> "The memorial speech I gave in Afghanistan, after Bryan and the other heroes passed, told a story of the ancient Spartan way of fighting. They fought in a formation called the 'phalanx.' I told the audience that this story was about all of the men of No Slack. The truth is, SSG Bryan Burgess was the sole inspiration for my words. Bryan was the glue of our phalanx. He was a natural leader of men, and it was easy to follow him. I have never been around a man who could say so much with so few words. His quiet confidence and leadership continue to inspire me to this day. If Bryan gave a simple nod, and half crooked smile, you knew everything was going to be ok. I was the commander of the company, and even I sought him out as a source of confidence. The love he showed for his men will never be matched, and we will all love him

forever. I pray this song helps in bringing you peace. It does for me."

God Bless
Tye L. Reedy
CPT, IN
Cougar 6

Capt. Reedy, who is now a major and teaches at West Point, and his wife, Alex, had a son and they named him after Bryan. Talk about being proud! Knowing that Bryan impressed his commanding officer that much still makes me smile!

My "little soldier" has since been honored by having four different boys named after him; Beau Bryan Reedy, Bryan Kraft, Bryan Jackson, and Bryan Allen. I hope I'm still around when they are old enough to want to learn about their namesake.

And from Specialist Brit "Doc" Jacobs about "Little Soldier:"

"Love this. It's all connected. In 5th grade, a descendant of Pocahontas gave my whole class a Native American name specific to each one of us. I told her I wanted to go on a mission when I grew up, and so she gave me the name 'Little Soldier'... Little did I know that I would be part of many missions, sharing that same name with many of my warrior brothers and sisters. I remember thinking this ... as if a sense of Deja vu fell over me ... I know that there is a certain Spirit about all of this ... I know that those who have fallen exemplified this Spirit ... And I know that those who live on continue to carry the same Spirit to the lives of many ... In this way the fallen are never forgotten ... Thanks to all the families who have raised such beautiful children. I know that the many lessons I have learned from your children began within the sacred walls of your own homes. Of course, you especially, fostered and initiated the Spirit of the "Little Soldier."

We had obtained several copies of the Little Soldier CD from Lee and I carried them with me on a flight out to Nashville. I was going to hand out a few to the No Slack soldiers at their reunion near Springfield, Tennessee.

Beth and I seemed to connect with the American Airlines flight attendants easily, and a conversation got started up with one about the CD. I wound up giving her five of the CDs to hand out to the flight crew. She came back just a minute later and sheepishly asked me if I happened to have a couple more of the CDs because Reba McEntire had taken her copies.

Reba was up in First Class and had seen the flight attendant carrying the CDs. Reba had asked what they were, because, you know, music and all that. So, the flight attendant told her about the CDs and us, and Reba asked if she could have a couple copies. The Flight attendant wasn't about to tell Reba McEntire "no," so she handed over two of the CDs.

I gave the flight attendant two more, and by now the majority of the main cabin was totally interested in what was going on. A few minutes later, here comes the flight attendant with one of the CDs and she said Reba wanted our autograph on a copy. I had one cd left in my carry on, so I took it and told the flight attendant I would trade my autograph for Reba's.

I now have a copy of the Little Soldier CD in Bryan's cabinet with Reba's autograph.

Sadly, Reba was long gone by the time we exited the plane.

We had several good experiences with American Airlines that involved Bryan. We were heading home after Bryan's funeral at Fort Campbell. Beth was clutching Bryan's American Flag to her chest, just daring anyone to tell her she couldn't hold it. Our seats were in back of the plane by the galley. We noticed after a few minutes that no one else was getting on the plane. We looked up and the Captain was headed toward us.

He sat down across from us and started asking questions about Bryan. He was a reservist and was about to be deployed to Afghanistan as a pilot. I shook his hand and gave him one of Bryan's poker chips and he said he had to go and let the other passengers on.

As the plane descended into DFW (Dallas-Ft. Worth), the Captain came on the intercom and told the passengers who we were and that we were on the back of the plane. He then asked if the other passengers would remain seated while we disembarked. I looked up to see the entire cabin looking back at us. It was a little intimidating.

We landed and sure enough, the passengers remained seated. We were half-way off the plane when they started applauding. One gentleman in First Class stood up as I passed him and he saluted us. I wordlessly shook his hand. We hugged the flight attendants and shook hands with the Captain and co-pilot and went to collect our luggage.

Several people came up to us at the luggage carrousel giving us condolences and hugs. It was very emotional for us, but it showed us that there are many, many people in this world who understand our sacrifice and it showed them that Gold Star parents are always among them; we're at the airport; we're in line at restaurants; we're in line at the grocery store; we're neighbors, and we're co-workers.

> There are many, many people in this world who understand our sacrifice … Gold Star parents are always among them; we're at the airport; we're in line at restaurants; we're in line at the grocery store; we're neighbors, and we're co-workers.

A USO volunteer at the Philadelphia Airport greeted us as we exited security. She literally took us by the hand and led us down the concourse. She stopped suddenly and asked me where my bag was. I looked around me like I had no idea what she was talking about. She told us to stay put and she ran back to security where she found my bag and calmly carried it with her all the way to the USO. I was amused to watch her "plowing the row" in front of us much like Sgt. Steed had done for us at the Kroger.

Our "family" quickly expanded beyond blood relations to include the men who had served with Bryan, the men and women of No Slack Task Force, medics, commanders, other Gold Star parents, spouses, and *The Hornet's Nest* movie crew.

As Beth and I toured America with the crew of *The Hornet's Nest* and met more No Slack soldiers, we also met many patriots and veterans who became like brothers and sisters to us.

One of those veterans is Major Andrew White of Frisco, Texas. We first met Major Andrew White at *The Hornet's Nest* screening at Southern Methodist University with the film's Executive Producers, David Salzberg, Jr. and Christian Tureaud, who is a SMU alumnus, and Command Sergeant Major (CSM) Chris Fields. After the film ended and just before Chris was to get up to speak he showed me a message from his wife, Debbie, on his cell phone. He had just received a message about a No Slack Soldier taking his own life. It was a harsh introduction for me into the knowledge that Bryan's men had brought the war—and all of its nightmares—home with them.

Major White addressed the assembly and he talked about that very thing: that our veterans were taking their own lives at the national rate of twenty-two suicides per day. A staggering statistic.

Chris Fields stood up and walked over to Major White and announced that one of his own men had just taken his own life.

You could literally have heard a pin drop in that auditorium.

As we were winding up the presentation and getting ready to dismiss, one of the SMU students, a basketball player, walked onto the floor and asked to speak. He addressed his coach and his teammates, telling them that he wanted to apologize to them for not giving 100 percent — and more — during their games. He talked about seeing how our soldiers gave their lives for each other and how it made him feel inadequate and unaccomplished as their teammate. It was a very moving testimonial coming from such a young athlete.

I have had several people ask me how Beth I can keep on giving back to other Gold Star parents and other organizations when we have already given and lost so much. When I think about Bryan and his brothers-in-arms fighting for each other, and when I see the absolute love and respect they have for my son, it makes it easier for me to give 100% of myself to make sure our fallen heroes are remembered and honored.

Beth and I were introduced to Major White, and he told us he hosted a radio show called Kilroy's Conversation on KVGI in Frisco and that he would very much like for us to be on his show sometime. We agreed and that became the start of a much-cherished relationship.

Our KVGI "family" grew quickly. Mark Wariner and his wife, Kim, Kevin Hodes and his wonderful family, along with Major White and his wife, Katie, have all become closer and dearer to us than simply as friends.

The same can be said of our Survivor Outreach Services (SOS) Coordinators. The website describes the SOS like this:

"The Survivor Outreach Services (SOS) Program exists to embrace and reassure Survivors that they are continually linked to the Military Family through a unified support program that enables them to remain an important part of the Military for as long as they desire. The Survivor Outreach Services (SOS) program is an Army-wide program which demonstrates our commitment to Families of the Fallen. SOS is a holistic and multi-agency approach to delivering services to Survivors by providing those services closest to where the Families live."

We describe our coordinators, Elisa and Chelsea, as "family." They attend events, have taken special training, conduct classes, and provide a special personal touch with art lessons and other crafts designed to help us relax and breathe, and they call us personally on Bryan's anniversary to let us know they are thinking about us. That is so very precious to us.

A surprise package in the mail introduced us to a group of people who very quickly became part of our "family." The package contained items from Wendy Tieck which she had received during her 2015 Chattanooga Iron Man 70.3 Triathlon. Wendy had run 13.1 miles, swam 1.2 miles, and biked 56 miles all for Bryan. Amy Cotta, the founder of Medals of Honor, received the items which included Wendy's jersey, swim cap, bracelets, finisher's medal, and race bib with Bryan's name, and mailed the items to us.

Beth and I were astounded at the fact that an athlete would do all of this for Bryan and then send their medal to his family. Wendy's race items are now in a shadow box hanging in our hallway. We have also received a Medals of Honor package from Carl Killian who completed the Little Debbie Iron Man in 2016. Wendy and Carl never met Bryan, or his family, yet they competed in and completed these incredible races and donated their race items to us.

We got to meet Amy Cotta at Fort Campbell at the annual Run for the Fallen and she convinced Beth that we could participate in the Bataan Memorial Death March at White Sands Missile Range in New Mexico. Since I had no idea what that entailed, I agreed.

The Bataan Memorial Death March marathon is exactly what their website says it is, "Much more than a marathon." I had read books and watched movies about the Death March in the Philippines during WWII, but after you actually meet, talk, and walk with some of the survivors, you really understand the sheer determination of the human spirit.

The Bataan Memorial Death March course is through desert sand. There are times on the course when you really need a walking stick to help you along. Staff of Honor in Kirbyville provided us with a very unique walking stick.

A good friend of ours who we had met through Snow Ball Express, Michele Carline, introduced us to Robert Wilson of Henry Brothers Knives. Robert creates unique staffs that are personalized for Veterans of the armed forces. When Michele asked Robert if he could create a staff for a Gold Star dad, Robert immediately took up the challenge. The staffs normally have a medallion of the branch the Veteran served with, along with their name and dates served.

The staff Robert created and presented to us is made of African purple heart wood. It bears the shield of the U.S. Army and has Bryan's name, rank, and dates engraved on the shaft. A polished .50 caliber shell casing acts as the foot of the staff. The very special and unique addition to Bryan's staff is his challenge coin embedded in the handle of the staff where you can see both sides of the coin.

When Robert presented us with Bryan's staff at the Kirbyville Veteran's Day in the Park event, he encouraged us to use it at the other events we attend. I did take it with me to the Bataan Memorial Death March, but I just couldn't subject it to the New Mexico desert, so I kept it in the special protective sleeve and only took it out for photos.

I took the staff with us to Stillwater, Oklahoma where some of our "family," Red Dirt Military Moms, conducts a twenty-two mile walk around Boomer Lake to bring awareness to the twenty-two veterans who commit suicide each day. Bob Evans, one of our No Slack family, his aunt Eva Turner, and his grandmother, Pat Apperson hold the annual event in September. I proudly displayed Bryan's staff and used it on the Boomer Lake trail.

A veteran's memorial is located on a jetty at the lake and I detoured from the path to take a moment to rest and reflect. As I turned back to the path, a gentleman wearing a No Slack cap was walking toward me. I had on a No Slack tee shirt and as he saw my shirt we both paused and he told me he was a Vietnam veteran and asked me if I had served with the unit. I told him Bryan's story.

I used to say, "Wow! What are the chances of that happening?" but it has happened so many times on so many different occasions that I have come to accept these seemingly coincidental happenings as normal occurrences.

"Family" also includes some of the most prestigious people on the most noble of missions.

In early 2015 I was contacted by Colonel James Stryker (Ret.) and Major General Joy Stevens (Ret.) who were working to have a monument created and placed on the Texas State Capitol grounds. The monument was to be called "The Price of Liberty." It consists of a soldier dressed in battle combat uniform who is holding his wife's hand while his right hand is grasped by a winged Goddess of Liberty who is taking him heavenward. The soldier's daughter stands stoically by her mother as she lovingly clasps a folded American Flag.

The symbolism of the memorial depicting the true price of liberty is instantly obvious to the observer.

Col. Stryker and Maj. Gen. Stevens asked me to join them at the State Capitol, to present their project to Senators and Representatives in hopes of getting a bill passed to have the memorial constructed on the Capitol Grounds. I heartily agreed to do so.

On March 15, 2015 armed with a scale model of the memorial, brochures, and a deep sense of pride and determination in our mission, we descended on the State Capitol. The day was long, but very fruitful.

~ Left to right: Author, State representative Debbie Riddle, Major General Joy Stevens, 2015

Governor Greg Abbott signed House Concurrent Resolution 70 on June 10, 2015 which allowed the memorial to be built (at no cost to the taxpayers) at the Capitol Complex. As a personal touch to the families who attended the memorial dedication in Austin on December 2, 2017, the Texas War Memorial team asked them to personalize bronze dog tags that would be placed in the base of the statue. Among the dog tags, which can be seen through a Plexiglas "window" in the base of the statue is a New Testament that was given to them by a Gold Star mother, and one of Bryan's challenge coins.

The impressive, eighteen-foot tall "Price of Liberty" dominates the intersection of San Jacinto Blvd and E 12th St near the Texas State Library and Archives Commission on the Capitol grounds.

~ "Price of Liberty" Texas Capitol Complex, December 02, 2017

~ The Legislative Team at the Texas Capitol with
Senator Larry Taylor, author of Senate Concurrent Resolution 24,
December 2, 2017

~ From left to right—Texas War Memorial Chairman Colonel (Retired)
James Stryker; Gold Star Dad Terry Burgess; Major General (Retired)
Joyce Stevens; Senator Larry Taylor; Christine Gilbreath, former Army
soldier and current president of the Texas National Guard Family
Support Foundation; Scott Gilbreth OIF (2 tours) and OEF Veteran; and
Ray Lindner, Executive Director of the Texas National Guard
Association of Texas and Treasurer of the Texas War Memorial.

Chapter 10
Who's to Blame?

There were other fears we became aware of. But these were not our fears. When we were attending the Eagle Remembrance Ceremony at Fort Campbell, May 31, 2011, we were seated at a huge round table with a gleaming white table cloth. We were by ourselves, but I could see toward the back of the room that the men of No Slack were all gathered together. I caught the eye of Sergeant First Class (SFC) Clint Lyons as he approached our table.

He squatted down beside me and whispered to me that the men wanted to talk to Beth and me, but they didn't know what to say to us. I told him no words were necessary; I just wanted to meet them.

Clint relayed the message and before we knew it our entire table was surrounded by No Slack soldiers! I met so many of them and heard so many stories it was hard to remember who told me what.

That was our first introduction to the men that had served with Bryan, and it was our first indication that some of them were afraid that we would blame them for Bryan's death. Some of them have told us that they weep because they should have acted sooner, run faster, done this or that, or just anything to keep that horrible day from happening. They second-guess themselves constantly and berate themselves for their "failure" to bring all their men home. These men carry that guilt with them every single day, regardless of what I or anyone else tells them. It's a dangerous cargo.

When we first met Mike Boettcher, we found out he was almost sheepish about meeting us because his son, Carlos, had returned home from Afghanistan and Bryan hadn't. Command Sgt. Major (CSM) Chris Fields and Colonel Joel "JB" Vowell were also wary of us until they were assured that we held no malice toward them for the outcome of Strong Eagle III. They were relieved to learn that Beth and I simply wanted to honor Bryan and his sacrifice as much as they did. We all remain close friends to this day.

We hold no blame or malice toward any of the men that served with No Slack during Operation Strong Eagle III. Blaming someone does no one any good. The group of people we wanted to hold responsible for Bryan's death and the death of his brothers were half a world away, out of our reach.

> We hold no blame or malice toward any of the men that served with No Slack during Operation Strong Eagle III. Blaming someone does no one any good.

Literally a few days after Qari Zia Rahman (known as QZR)—the man who was the reason for Operation Strong Eagle III— had been killed, I began receiving text messages and emails that simply said, "We got him." I held no remorse for the death of a man whose entire life had been dedicated to killing Americans and American soldiers.

> I held no remorse for the death of a man whose entire life had been dedicated to killing Americans and American soldiers.

There are still some things that I blame myself for ... but no one needs to be admitted to that three-ring circus. I know Bryan would still be carrying "survivor's guilt" with him right now because of the incidents which he had survived that others had not. We learned that he had survived some horrific incidents in Iraq by sheer happenstance while his teammates did not.

On one incident, Bryan had switched a vehicle search post with a fellow soldier and that soldier had been killed when a car bomb went off during that shift.

On another incident, Bryan was a rear guard of a team who was killed when a bomb detonated during a building search.

In December of 2004, Bryan had just exited the mess tent at FOB Marez in Mosul, Iraq just as a suicide bomber walked in the opposite door. Twenty-two people were killed and sixty-six were injured in the blast.

I had observed dark shadows in Bryan's eyes the last time I saw him. He used to accuse me of playing "Twenty Questions" with him on his leaves, but I did not dare ask about the ghosts I could see in his eyes.

Maybe I should have asked.

There are organizations which only recognize a Gold Star as one who has had a family member killed in action. We have met so very many parents who tell us their soldier was killed during a training exercise, or was killed in an accident on a military base, or was killed in an automobile accident while home on leave. We have even heard the tragic story of a soldier that contracted—and died from—small pox from the inoculation he was given before deployment.

And then there are the suicides. Currently the national statistic states that twenty-two veterans take their own life each day. These are veterans from all wars, not just the Global War on Terror.

Not one single solider has ever come home from deployment who is the same son or daughter who left home. No one comes back the same.

The changes I saw in Bryan ran deep. I could see that plainly. I could not see the scars on his heart and soul, and he would probably have never told me what caused those scars, even if I had asked him.

Getting soldiers to talk about their experiences while deployed is one of the hardest things for a spouse or a parent. The soldier will usually reply with, "I was just doing my job."

I do not know, and I don't allow myself to dwell on wondering what would have happened to Bryan if he had survived and stayed in the Army. He wanted to make the Army his career. He was good at it and his men dearly loved him, and they literally followed him into hell.

Multiple deployments take a horrible toll on a soldier's life and mentality. Our sons and daughters are raised in a country that shares and respects Christian values where life is recognized as a gift of God. When they have to face an enemy who has no morals and no regard for human life, our soldiers, our sons and daughters, our children, have to shove their own morals into a deep, dark recess of their mind.

Terry Burgess

When our children come home from deployment, they are no longer children. They are men and women who have faced an armed enemy. They have had to make life or death decisions in a split second. And they have to live with those decisions for the rest of their lives.

Sadly, and tragically, some of our children cannot bear to live with those memories stuck in their head, and they see only one way to get them out.

Chapter 11
Our Address Book Changed

During one of our retreats, I dreamt I was standing among my family and I suddenly just shattered like a piece of glass being dropped onto stone. My family immediately called on friends and neighbors to come help put me back together. They reassembled me as best as they could, then they stepped back to admire their handiwork while saying, "Look! He's all put back together just like he was!"

Yet I was afraid to move a muscle because I knew any little bump or sudden movement would break me into a thousand tiny pieces again.

Family and friends may think they know how to "fix" you. They may try to say all the right things in the hope of getting their "old" Terry back again. The societal stigma is that six months of grieving should be plenty of time to "get over" the loss of a loved one, let alone six years. A family member once told me that I was too obsessed with Bryan's death and the film *The Hornet's Nest*, and that I needed to move on and do something positive with my life.

That "old" Terry died the same day as Bryan. And the most positive thing I could do to live up to Bryan's sacrifice was to share his story.

Beth shares her feelings about how Bryan's death not only affected her, but tested the strength of our marriage:

> "I didn't just lose Bryan; I also lost the man who had been my husband. The wonderful man whom I had married and who I knew without a doubt I could always lean on—no matter what happened—was gone. In his place was someone who was completely shattered and was now looking to me to carry both of us through the nightmare that had just erupted in our lives.

> "This was one of the biggest challenges we had ever faced together and now had to learn to navigate. Our marriage had ended and a new one had taken its place. We had to learn how to relate to each other, how to talk to each other, and how to be there for each other in a whole new way.

"We are still navigating our way through this 'new normal.' So, when people ask how long we have been married, instead of saying twenty-five years, I want to say seven years because this is our second, or rather, our 'after' marriage."

That was around the time we noticed that our address book was changing. We were making connections with people who shared our grief and people who "got it." We were weeding out the people that had told us we had mourned long enough, or that we really needed to seek professional help to get over Bryan's death.

> We were making connections with people who shared our grief and people who "got it."

Our address book was filling up with the names of military men and women, soldiers who had served with Bryan, Army personnel, organizations dedicated to Gold Stars, families affected by military suicides, and true patriots. Instead of simply containing casual acquaintances, business people, or friends of friends, our contacts now included Medal of Honor recipients, Tuskegee Airmen, sports legends, entertainers, musicians, movie stars, TV personalities, politicians, and CEOs. I still have the business cards of the Lt. Col. and of the minister who visited us the morning of Bryan's death.

In 2014, I had some challenge coins created to honor Bryan, and I have given away almost 1,000 of them. Bryan's coin, redesigned and perfected by Joseph "Booch" Buccini and Clifford "Scoop" Davis of Still Serving Promos, has Bryan's portrait, name, rank, his birth-date and his KIA date on the front and the reverse has the words "Never Forget" under the Soldier's Battlefield cross along with a Bronze Star medal and the U.S. Army shield.

The history of the challenge coin is sometimes varied but it comes down to this: a medallion or coin that represents either a military branch of service, a specific unit in a specific branch, a special organization or a person — living or deceased — in a particular organization. The "challenge" comes when several members of a specific organization or branch come together and the members challenge each other to produce the coin that had been presented to them.

It's very humbling to run into someone years later and have them pull Bryan's coin out of their pocket or wallet.

As Beth and I were leaving Snowball Express in Dallas, I noticed a police cruiser following closely behind me. Snowball Express is a four-day extravaganza honoring the children of fallen soldiers with an all-expense paid trip, including chartered flights, magic shows, day trips to area attractions and a hotel set up to cater to their every need. We volunteer every year and get very little sleep during those four days, so I started asking Beth if I had run a stop light or something. She said she had not noticed if I had. The officer followed me all the way from downtown Dallas, down I 35 to U.S. 67 for about ten miles, where he pulled up alongside of me, no lights or sirens, and he motioned for me to pull over. I complied.

The officer stopped behind us, but he came up to the passenger side of our truck which seemed unusual. Beth rolled her window down and the officer was holding up one of Bryan's coins!

I had met the officer years before at the Tribute to Fallen Soldiers motorcycle ride conducted by Warren Williamson out of Oregon. I had presented the officer with one of Bryan's coins because he had been our escort for the ride. He had seen our truck coming out of Dallas and he simply wanted to let me know that he still carried Bryan's coin.

I cannot explain how that level of respect makes me feel.

So, if you are carrying one of Bryan's coins right now, please know how much that means to me and our family!

Challenge Coin (front)

Challenge Coin (back)

Chapter 12
Coming Home

Our niece, Kamille, and her then fiancé, Bradley, volunteered to housesit for us while we were traveling during March and April of 2011. Bradley was attending college at the time and he told his professors that he needed to take some time off due to a death in the family. To their credit, they let Bradley take all the time he needed to care for Beth and me. They took care of our two cats, Beast and Wally, they watered plants, collected mail, answered emails, paid bills, and fielded phone calls from the press.

We found out that once Bryan's death became public, so did our lives. The press called almost everyone we knew at the time. They got hold of my dad in Clyde; they called Beth's sisters at their work place.

Our privacy was gone. We were now living in the "glass house of grief."

Tiffany, Bryan's widow, decided early on that all press contacts needed to have one contact point. It was a wise decision that would save us a lot of heartache and misunderstandings. Somehow, the press decided that Bryan had two daughters instead of a daughter and a son. In spite of Tiffany's efforts, information still got miscommunicated.

Gathering with the other five families on that cold, rainy morning of March 31 there at Dover Air Force Base to wait for the transport plane that was bringing our son's remains home to the United States, was almost overwhelming. There was a palpable feeling of tension mixed with the air of nervous anticipation.

There was a huge room in the west wing of the Fisher House where we congregated. At that point none of us knew what to say to each other. We were still strangers to each other with our grief being the only thing we had in common. It was an uncomfortable comfort to see them all.

> It was an uncomfortable comfort to see them all.

The family of one of the soldiers killed, SFC Ofren Arrechaga, sat apart. We could hear their CAO translating English into Spanish for Ofren's mother and father. The Arrechagas and the Adamskis would later on become closer than brothers and sisters to us.

The Fisher House volunteers came into the room with coffee and cookies and pastries, and more importantly, gloves, coats, and scarves. It was cold outside and none of us had packed warm clothes.

The sugar and caffeine gave us all some much-needed energy and we began to mingle and talk with the other families, finding out the names of the other five No Slack soldiers who were coming home with Bryan:

Sergeant First Class Ofren Arrechaga, 28 years old, of Hialeah, Florida

Staff Sergeant Frank E. Adamski III, 26 years old, of Moosup, Connecticut

Specialist Jameson L Lindskog, 23 years old, of Pleasanton, California

Specialist Dustin J. Feldhaus, 20 years old, of Glendale, Arizona

Private First Class Jeremy P. Falukner, 23 years old, of Griffin, Georgia

A major came into the room and told us how the Dignified Transfer was going to take place. The Burgess Family would remain in the hall while the other families went out onto the tarmac to see the Dignified Transfer. I stepped forward and asked, "Why?" Tiffany took me by the arm and said, "Dad, I told you it's because of our press blackout. The press will be on the tarmac for the other families. I didn't want them there for Bryan." I had either missed or totally forgotten that Tiffany had told me that. So, we waited while the other five families filed out of the room and onto the tarmac.

It wasn't too long until the outside door opened and another major said, "It's time." We filed outside and boarded a waiting shuttle in silence. The driver of the shuttle stood at attention as we boarded. Knowing that his salute was intended for the sacrifice of my son made my eyes fill with tears.

Besides the singular jet sitting on the runway, I noticed a cadre of soldiers standing at attention holding a salute. We walked past them out to the jet.

Bryan's casket sat in the cargo doorway of a huge four-engine chartered jet. One corner of the American flag had come loose from his casket and a soldier jumped into the hold, quickly secured it, and snapped a salute to the ground crew.

Seven soldiers, known as the Army Carry Team, dressed in fatigues and wearing black berets and white gloves, marched slowly over to the jet. The elevator lowered

Bryan's casket to ground level. I thought we might be able to walk over to it, touch it, or something. But we were kept back twenty-five feet. It was bitter cold out there. A soldier draped a blanket around Beth's shoulders at some point.

Bryan's casket was eased from the trolley into the hands of the soldiers, being passed pair-by-pair until all six soldiers supported the casket. Three more soldiers stood at attention as the casket was painstakingly marched to a waiting van.

~ Dover Air Force Base, March 31, 2011

I remember thinking how absolutely silent it was. If not for all of us sniffing and holding back tears, I would have thought I'd gone deaf.

Our eyes tracked the soldier's movement as Bryan's casket was carried over to a waiting van. My eyes swept over the cadre still standing at attention and still holding a salute. Bryan was loaded into the van and driven over to a huge building where two more soldiers stood at attention on either side of the open door. I watched until the van was out of sight. I looked around and saw that I was the last one standing out on the tarmac. The cadre was still at attention, still saluting when I last saw them.

We learned that Bryan's body would now be in the hands of Mortuary Affairs. I knew what that meant, but I didn't know *what* that meant. We have since met Gerry and Christina Smith through Amy Cotta and her organization, Medals of Honor: http://medalsofhonor.org/.

Christina then served in Mortuary Affairs. Learning of the extreme care, honor, and reverence given to Bryan by this elite group makes me so very proud. It's a difficult job, and the personnel are rotated out regularly. But it is a job they will carry with them forever.

Going home would have been horrible except for the fact that we were escorted by Sgt. Rose and we knew that Kamille and Bradley were already there with Beast and Wally. We walked into a warm, well-lit house with the wonderful aroma of Italian food wafting in the air. Kamille and Bradley had prepared a meal for us, replete with soft candle light and a set table. We encouraged Sgt. Rose to dine with us, but he had to report back to Fort Hood. He gently informed us that the following days were not going to be any easier. I gave him a hug, he departed, and we sat down to eat.

"Home" had forever been changed for us.

"Home" had forever been changed for us.

After Beth's mother passed away, she and her sisters were faced with the chore of cleaning out their parents' home. Going through someone else's personal things makes you realize how much stuff you can accumulate in a lifetime. Sorting through all the things you've bought, collected, and were given gives you a strange sense of mortality.

We have a special cabinet that houses Bryan's ashes, war medals, personal items, and gifts from friends and relatives. We have an entire shelf of Starbucks mugs that Tiffany and Bryan gave us from different countries and cities.

Everyone has things in their home. We have essentials, we have decorations, and toys and electronics for entertainment. A grieving parent will see all these *things* as simply that. They are just things. Meaningless, pointless things. But let them just try to throw away a sock that their child once wore, or a toothbrush that they once used, and these things suddenly become as beautiful and meaningful as a religious relic.

We did not have nice, expensive cameras when Bryan was growing up so we do not have high-definition photos of him at a young age. We didn't have smartphones or video recorders. We have some nice photos that we have preserved and scanned and uploaded and shared.

There is nobody walking around telling parents, "Oh! You should be taking professional photos of your children now because they may be killed some day!" That's not how it works. I have precious memories of Bryan that are strictly my own. These are my treasures. I remember being at Six Flags Over Texas with Bryan when he was maybe eight years old. It was the end of a wonderful day and we had stopped in one of the gift shops so Bryan could pick out a souvenir, and I actually remember thinking to myself, *these are the good old days.* I even remember that the song "Jesse" by Carly Simon was playing over the loud speakers. To this day that song triggers that memory. I have no photos of Bryan from that day. What I do have is a precious memory of my son smiling at me as he carried his own treasure out to our car.

I have many regrets from the times I said "No!" to Bryan when I could just have easily said "Yes!" But I was being a parent. I was doing what I thought was right at the time for my son.

Even though I smashed a ceramic plate with the word *regret* written on it, I will probably carry those regrets to my grave. Beth and many dear friends have told me that my regrets will help keep me humble in my ongoing mission to honor Bryan.

And in the end? I cannot even fathom the end. Grief has no ending.

At one of the functions we attended the guest speaker said that military families hold their breath during deployments.

Gold Star families never get to exhale.

Some of my tears, however, have become smiles, especially when I see Bryan's name on a race bib, or on a brick in a memorial garden, or his face on a poster.

Never stop honoring your heroes.
Share their stories.
Tell their names.
Shed those tears.
And smile.

"Chariots"

Through the wind, below the sand, around me is the hush
I feel the souls, but broken bones have quickly turned to
dust
Your chariot awaits…
Your chariot awaits…
Can't numb the pain, but I am numb to what's going on
Frozen thoughts are trapping me,
But the world it still goes round
My chariot awaits…
My chariot awaits…

Sometimes the promises we make
Are the hardest ones to keep
But I'll be damned if I let you down
You've always lifted me
Your chariot awaits…
Your chariot awaits…
I slip away, but I hear the noise,
The chaos in this place
But I'll be fine, I've lived my life
I would never change a thing
My chariot awaits…

"Chariots"

Tell my mother, that I love her
Say "I'm sorry" to my brother
Scream "I love you" to my baby
Share my story,
Don't forget me.

About the Author

Terry Burgess is a Magna Cum Laude graduate of Tarleton State University. He and his wife, Elisabeth, moved to Fort Worth, Texas in 1999. They both have worked in the financial and banking industry as business analysts.

Terry is the former president of the Chasing Gold Toastmasters Club, an ordained minister, an author of five fiction novels, and the current Vice President of Gold Star Family Relations for The Apache Warrior Foundation. Elisabeth is the current Treasurer of The Apache Warrior Foundation.

Terry and Beth created their own registered 501 (c) 3 non-profit organization, Gold Star Parents Retreat, which provides a cost-free weekend retreat to any Gold Star parent.

Please visit: **www.goldstarparentsretreat.org**

Their logo consists of the Gold Star pin on an Oak Leaf with the American Flag in the background.

Oak leaves are commonly used as military symbols of strength and resilience.

They are members of The American Legion and the North Texas Patriot Guard Riders.

The Burgesses became a Gold Star Family on March 29, 2011 when their son, Army Staff Sergeant Bryan Burgess of the 101st Airborne, was killed during a Taliban Ambush in Kunar Province, Afghanistan. It was Bryan's third tour.

In 2013-2014 Terry and Beth toured the United States with *The Hornet's Nest*, a feature film that includes actual footage of Bryan and his final tour of duty.

Their sole motivation in writing *When Our Blue Star Turned Gold* is to tell Bryan's story to honor his sacrifice, and inspire other Gold Star Families to tell their own stories, so many people will understand and truly appreciate the high costs of freedom.

Terry and Elisabeth are available for speaking engagements and events which honor the military and their members' commitments to serve and to sacrifice.

Contact them through **www.GoldStarParent.com**

Permissions and Credits
In Order of Appearance

Phil Taylor – The American Fallen Soldier Project

David Salzberg, Jr.

Christian Tureaud

Maj. Gen. Joy Stevens (Ret.)

Col. James Stryker (Ret.)

Casey McEuin

Karl Monger

SFC Michael Schlitz – U.S. Army (Retired)

MSG Blair Anderson (Retired)

Sgt. Nate Allen

Tiffany Kasinger-Burgess

Lt. Col. Eberhart

Reverend Mark Moore

SFC Newton Rose, U.S. Army Casualty Assistance Officer (CAO)

Gen. Jeff Colt

Sgt. Brent Schneider

Brandi Burgess

PGR

SFC Clint Lyons

Johnny Shotwell

Christine Gilbreath

Debi Barber, Francene Ferrante, Elisabeth Burgess

Kelly Castonguay

Gene Sweeny

Carl and Carol Wallin

Cherry Yvonne

Brent Dones

Bob Vincent

Ron White

Mic Stephens

JoAnn Stephens

Ken Stephens

David Roberts

Josephine Riley, John and Lisa Skier

Warren Williamson

Kathy Dunn –"Release" Katsuz Kreations

Jon "Weasel" Meleshenko

Doc Jacobs

SSG. Mark Burrell

Mike Boettcher

Carlos Boettcher

Michael Trella

Maj. Tye Reedy

Lee Shaw

Annika Horne

Maj. Andrew White (Ret.)

CSM Chris Fields

Mark Wariner

Kevin Hodes

Elisa Marquis

Chelsea Daughtry

Amy Cotta

Wendy Tiek

Carl Killian

Robert Wilson

Michele Carline

Bob Evans

Eva Turner

Pat Apperson

Lt. Col. "JB" Vowell

Joseph "Booch" Buccini

Clifford "Scoop" Davis

Gerry and Christina Smith

Appendix: Resources

Organizations Dedicated to Serving Gold Star Families

Chapter 1

> The American Fallen Soldiers Project
> https://americanfallensoldiers.com/
> Phil Taylor creates personal portraits.

> Fisher House Foundation https://www.fisherhouse.org/
> https://www.fisherhouse.org/programs/houses/house-
> locations/delaware-fisher-house-for-families-of-the-fallen/

Chapter 2

> Patriot Guard Riders
> https://www.patriotguard.org/

Chapter 3

> Flags For Fallen Vets
> http://www.flagsforfallenvets.com/

Resources

Designs On Demand
https://www.designsondemand.com/
Creates unique dog tags for families of the fallen

Chapter 4

The Hornet's Nest movie
http://thehornetsnestmovie.com/

Chapter 5

Afghanistan Memory Wall — Ron White:
https://Americasmemory.com

American Airlines Sky Ball
https://skyballinfo.com/

Carry The Load
http://www.carrytheload.org
Dallas Memorial March

The Riley Run
https://runsignup.com/Race/TX/Tolar/RileyRun5K
The Riley Run is in memory of Sgt. 1st Class Riley G. Stephens and
benefits a Memorial Scholarship fund in his name for
graduates of Tolar High School.

Suck It Up Ruck
https://www.facebook.com/SuckitupRuck/
22k of road marching to honor 3 heroes lost. 22k to bring
awareness to the 22 suicides a day of veterans/active duty.

Bataan Memorial Death March
http://bataanmarch.com/
The Bataan Memorial Death March is a challenging march through the high desert terrain of the White Sands Missile Range. The memorial march is conducted in honor of the heroic service members who defended the Philippine Islands during World War II, sacrificing their freedom, health, and, in many cases, their very lives.

The Marine Corps Marathon
http://www.marinemarathon.com/
Annually ranked as one of the largest marathons in the US and the world, the MCM has been recognized as "Best Marathon in the Mid-Atlantic," "Best for Families" and "Best for Beginners."

Chapter 6
Gold Star Parent's Retreat
https://goldstarparentsretreat.org/

The Riley Run
https://www.rileyrun.org/

Carry The Load
http://www.carrytheload.org/site/PageServer?pagename=home

Watermelon Run For the Fallen
http://watermelonrftf.org/
Watermelon Run for the Fallen is the nation's largest 5k run/walk/roll dedicated to recognizing the sacrifice of our military members who have been lost as a result of our current conflicts.

Warren Williamson
Tribute To Fallen Soldiers Northwest
http://tributetofallensoldiers.com/

Chapter 7

KVGI Radio
https://kvgiradio.com/

Texas War Memorial
http://texaswarmemorial.com/
Our mission is to build, place, and provide an endowment for
future maintenance and upkeep of "The Price of Liberty"
Memorial Statue at the Texas Capitol. Major General (Retired) Joy
Stevens, Colonel (Retired) James Stryker
Texas State Representative Debbie Riddle

The Dixon Center
http://dixoncenter.org/
As a center providing leadership, tested solutions, research, and
training Dixon Center is dedicated to helping organizations and
communities improve the quality of life of veterans and military
families.

Chapter 8

Stay The Course
http://www.staythecourse.vet/
A non-profit organization providing evidence-based therapies to
individuals, couples, and families at little or no cost

22Kill

http://www.22kill.com/

22KILL provides traditional and non-traditional therapies for service members and their families. Our focus is on empowerment and helping individuals find a sense of purpose after service. This includes all services: Military, Police, Fire, and EMS

Chapter 9

Snowball Express

https://www.snowballexpress.org/

Serving the children of our fallen Military Heroes

Still Serving Promos

https://www.stillservingpromos.com/

Tribute to Fallen Soldiers Northwest

http://tributetofallensoldiers.com/

A mission to honor America's Fallen Heroes

Chapter 10

Survivor Outreach Services

https://www.armymwr.com/programs-and-services/personal-assistance/survivor-outreach

Offers access to support, information, and services, closest to where you live, when you need it and for as long as you need it.

BrothersKeepers

http://brothers-keepers.org/

Healing Veterans & First Responders

One Family at a Time

Red Dirt Military Moms
https://www.warriorsforfreedom.org/rdmm/

Apache Warrior Foundation
https://apachewarriorfoundation.com/
The mission of the Apache Warrior Foundation is to support the
AH-64 Attack Helicopter community by giving Honor to our
brotherhood forged in blood, Heal ourselves and our families, and
Educate the public of the skill sacrifice that keeps our country free.

Medals Of Honor
http://medalsofhonor.org/
National Awareness Campaign to honor fallen military
and their families

1Lt. Robbie Welch Memorial Run
https://www.1ltwelchrunforourheroes.org/
To forevermore preserve the memory of those like 1LT Robert
"Robby" Welch III, who selflessly and proudly served their
country, standing for liberty and freedom, and, in doing so, paid
the ultimate sacrifice to defend her and her people.

Heroes Race
http://www.theheroesrace.org/
Recognizing local everyday community heroes

Dog Tag Brewing
https://www.dogtagbrewing.org/
A nonprofit that works with Gold Star Families to honor
America's Fallen Warriors

Honor Wine
http://www.honorwinery.com/
Dedicated to the men and women who proudly serve our country.

Team Fastrax Warrior Weekend to Remember
http://warriorwtr.com/
Blue Skies for the Good Guys and Gals Warrior Foundation's mission is to honor our nation's veterans, Purple Heart Warriors and the families of fallen heroes by providing enriching, life changing experiences that facilitate new friendships and emotional healing.

Gold Star Families Memorial
http://hwwmohf.org/monument-overview.html
The purpose of the Gold Star Families Memorial Monument is to honor Gold Star Families, preserve the memory of the fallen, and stand as a stark reminder that Freedom is not free.

Global War on Terror Memorial Foundation
https://www.gwotmemorialfoundation.org/

Project RELO
http://www.projectrelo.org/
Project RELO missions provide superlative leadership training. Yet, even more importantly, participants develop a deep understanding about the character, quality, and full extent of our veterans' skills. And with this understanding comes appreciation, and a desire to hire more of our former military members into our respective organizations. Project RELO then continues its veteran advocacy beyond the missions by helping firms establish, Or improve existing military hiring programs.

Surviving Families of Fallen Warriors
https://www.sffwtexas.org/

Wreaths Across America
https://www.wreathsacrossamerica.org/
Each December on National Wreaths Across America Day,
our mission to Remember, Honor and Teach is carried out by
coordinating wreath-laying ceremonies at Arlington National
Cemetery, as well as at more than 1,400 additional locations in
all 50 U.S. states, at sea and abroad.

Run for the Fallen
https://www.honorandremember.org/run-for-the-fallen/

Honor and Remember
https://www.honorandremember.org/

Honoring The Sacrifice
http://honoringthesacrifice.com/
The Honoring the Sacrifice Foundation was formed in 2013 by
wounded United States Army Sgt. Andrew Smith (retired) and his
wife, Tori. Together with a dedicated team of volunteers, the
husband and wife duo are assisting service members and their
families, just as they have been supported during their journey.

Heroes on the Water
https://heroesonthewater.org/
A veteran's charity that applies a simple solution to a complex
issue—giving veterans, first responders and their families a path
to a successful life.

Refuge In Grief
http://www.refugeingrief.com/

Stepping Forward in Grief
https://steppingforwardstudy.org/
Stepping Forward in Grief (SFG) is a study that develops and tests an innovative, mobile and web guide-supported application designed to promote adaptation to loss, as well as encourage grief integration in a geographically dispersed community of military families who have experienced loss.

Go Ruck
www.goruck.com

Country Music Remembers
http://countrymusicremembers.com/
Share your hero on their memory wall

Gold Star Family Registry
http://www.goldstarfamilyregistry.com/

Wear Blue: Run to Remember
http://www.wearblueuntoremember.org/

Texas Hunters for Heroes
https://texashuntersforheroes.org/

Gold Star Dirt
https://goldstardirt.org/
Telling the stories of fallen service members through the voices of their Gold Star families

GallantFew Revolutionary Veteran Support Network:
Karl Monger
www.gallantfew.org

Evermore
www.live-evermore.org
Evermore is here to improve the lives of families who experienced the death of a child, whether young or old, from accidents, violence, suicide, war, illness, natural causes, or disasters. We are working to marshal the full support of communities and society by providing bereaved families with all the resources, opportunities and societal supports our nation has to offer.

Author Notes of Appreciation

Bryan's family owes a debt of gratitude to so very many people who have shown them immeasurable love and support. We have mentioned many of them in the book and in the Special Thanks section below, but the list is incomplete. We did not intentionally omit anyone.

We lost a son, but we have gained a nation-full of people who truly have become our Family, and we know there are many more yet to come.

Special Thanks

Ernesto Casas
Nicolas and Michelle Beuke
Trinnie Schley
Mike, Debbie, and Justin Elliott
Matthew Miller
Toni Finch Russell
Randy Stillinger
Alin Bijan
David Keuhner

Mike Cagle
Boot Campaign
Ron, Janece and J.R. Hill
LaRue Walls
Peggy Bidwell
Debbie Woods
Linda Traylor
Monica Bishop
Pamela Harrison
Kim Mitchell
Our entire BrothersKeepers Family
Alexander Hillburn and *That's All Brother*
Jon Laureles and the Allmon-Burgess VFW Post 12152
Beverly Williams
J.R. Rowley and the Riley Stephens VFW Post 7835
Lynn Toomer and the VFW Post 6872
Hal Cleveland, USN, (Ret.)
Andy Asberry
David Bowers
Terry Carlile
Burleson Rocks
No Slack Nation
LTC Allen Hahn
Penny Belcourt
Apache Warrior Foundation
Senator Brian Birdwell
Representative Dan Flynn
Shannon Schneider – *Go Ruck*
Michael Reagan
Ken Pridgeon
David Butterbaugh
Eddie Contreas

Bobby Henline
Michael Jernigan
Shilo Harris
Cory Collier
Dave Bray
Jeff Senour and CTS
Jon Lunkwicz
Wayne Boze Funeral Home
Cliff Sosamon
Mike Meeker
Christine Kolenik
Jason Mergott
Gratitude Entertainment
Col Christian Cabiness
Rick Irving
Jack Barnes, CPO USN (Ret.) and America –
        Celebrate, Honor & Serve
Dog Tag Brewing
Buck Kern
Phil Vandel
Matt Snook
Diana Nagy
Wendy Slaten
Camyle Coleman
Leslie McClendon
Stephanie Freeman
Metroport Veterans Association
Michael Brauer
Our entire 22Kill Family
Doug Pruitt
Brent Casey
Chad Graham

Larry Shatto
Latoya Silmon
Dan Lombardo, Jr.
Tempa Sherrill and Stay The Course
Tarah Toney
Aaron Bartal and *Running To Honor*
Craig and Donna Kleman
Surviving Families of Fallen Warriors
Joe James
Alvarado High School Baseball
Vanderbilt University
David Hart
John Hart
Team Fastrax Warrior Weekend to Remember
Ria Hale
George Lutz
Honor and Remember
Bobby Withrow
Remembering Our Fallen From Texas
Museum of the American GI
David Vargo
Dave's Military Display
The 2014 Red Oak Jr. High for the Central Texas Chapter of *The Home of the Brave Quilt Project*
The Northwood Gratitude & Honor Memorial
Joyal Mulheron
Cindy Dodson
Jim Palmersheim
Tal Milan
Jose Tavera
Joel Tavera
Dave Griminger

Author Notes of Appreciation

Deb Hanson
Jane Horton
John Cremering
Jarrod Stover
Anne Gialdini
Sgt. Shane Shelton

*****

CPSIA information can be obtained
at www.ICGtesting.com
Printed in the USA
LVHW030628231118
597929LV00002B/242/P